The Gnostic Scriptures

History, Theology, and the Sacred Feminine

By

Joseph B. Lumpkin

Joseph B. Lumpkin

Gnostic Scriptures

History, Theology, and the Sacred Feminine

Fifth Estate Publishers,

Post Office Box 116, Blountsville, AL 35031.

First Printing June 2006

Cover Design by An Quigley

Printed on acid-free paper

Library of Congress Control No: 2006929875

ISBN: 1933580267

Fifth Estate 2006

Joseph B. Lumpkin

Introduction

"Gnosticism: A system of religion mixed with Greek and Oriental philosophy of the 1st through 6th centuries A.D. Intermediate between Christianity and paganism, Gnosticism taught that knowledge rather than faith was the greatest good and that through knowledge alone could salvation be attained."

Webster's Dictionary

The word Gnostic is based on the Greek word "Gnosis," which means "knowledge." The "Gnosis" is the knowledge of the ultimate, supreme God and his spirit, which is contained within us all. It is this knowledge that allows one to transcend this material world with its falsities and spiritual entrapments and ascend into heaven to be one with God.

For centuries the definition of Gnosticism has in itself been a point of confusion and contention within the religious community. This is due in part to the ever-broadening application of the term and the fact that various sects of Gnosticism existed as the theology evolved and began to merge into what became mainstream Christianity.

Even though Gnosticism continued to evolve, it is the theology in place at the time that the Gnostic Gospels were

Joseph B. Lumpkin

written that should be considered and understood before attempting to render or read a translation. To do otherwise would make the translation cloudy and obtuse.

It becomes the duty of both translator and reader to understand the ideas being espoused and the terms conveying those ideas. A grasp of theology, cosmology, and relevant terms is necessary for a clear transmission of the meaning within the text in question.

With this in mind, we will briefly examine Gnostic theology, cosmology, and history. We will focus primarily on Gnostic sects existing in the first through fourth centuries A.D. since it is believed most Gnostic Gospels were written during that time. It was also during that time that reactions within the emerging Christian orthodoxy began to intensify.

The downfall of many books written on the topic of religion is the attempt to somehow remove history and people from the equation. History shapes religion because it shapes the perception and direction of religious leaders. Religion also develops and evolves in an attempt to make sense of the universe as it is seen and understood at the time. Thus, to truly grasp a religious concept it is important to know the history, people, and cosmology of the time. These areas are not separate but are continually interacting. This is how the information in this book will be presented to the reader.

A Brief Lesson in Gnosticism

The roots of the Gnosticism may pre-date Christianity. Similarities exist between Gnosticism and the wisdom and mystery cults found in Egypt and Greece. Gnosticism contains the basic terms and motifs of Plato's cosmology as well as the mystical qualities of Buddhism. Plato was steeped in Greek mythology, and the Gnostic creation myth has elements owing to this. Both cosmology and mysticism within Gnosticism present an interpretation of Christ's existence and teachings, thus, Gnostics are considered to be a Christian sect. Gnostic followers are urged to look within themselves for the truth and the Christ spirit hidden, asleep in their souls. The battle cry can be summed up in the words of the Gnostic Gospel of Thomas, verse 3:

> *Jesus said: If those who lead you say to you: Look, the Kingdom is in the sky, then the birds of the sky would enter before you. If they say to you: It is in the sea, then the fish of the sea would enter ahead of you. But the Kingdom of God exists within you and it exists outside of you. Those who come to know (recognize) themselves will find it, and when you come to know yourselves you will become known and you will realize that you are the children of the Living Father. Yet if you do not come to know*

7

*yourselves then you will dwell in poverty and it will be you who
are that poverty.*

Paganism was a religious traditional society in the
Mediterranean leading up to the time of the Gnostics. Centuries
after the conversion of Constantine, mystery cults worshipping
various Egyptian and Greco-Roman gods continued. These
cults taught that through their secret knowledge worshippers
could control or escape the mortal realm. The Gnostic doctrine
of inner knowledge and freedom may have part of its roots
here. The concept of duality and inner guidance taught in
Buddhism added to and enforced Gnostic beliefs, as we will see
later.

The belief systems of Plato, Buddha, and paganism
melted together, spread, and found a suitable home in the
mystical side of the Christian faith as it sought to adapt and
adopt certain Judeo-Christian beliefs and symbols.

Like modern Christianity, Gnosticism had various
points of view that could be likened to Christian
denominations of today. Complex and elaborate creation myths
took root in Gnosticism, being derived from those of Plato.
Later, the theology evolved and Gnosticism began to shed
some of its more unorthodox myths, leaving the central theme
of inner knowledge or gnosis to propagate.

The existence of various sects of Gnosticism, differing creation stories, along with the lack of historical documentation, has left scholars in a quandary about exactly what Gnostics believed. Some have suggested that the Gnostics represented a free thinking and idealistic movement much like that of the "Hippie" movement active in the United States during the 1960's.

Just as the "Hippie" movement in the U.S. influenced political thought, some early sects of Gnostics began to exert direct influence on the Christian church and its leadership.

Although it appears that there were several sects of Gnosticism, we will attempt to discuss the more universal Gnostic beliefs along with the highlights of the major sects.

Gnostic cosmology, (which is the theory of how the universe is created, constructed, and sustained), is complex and very different from orthodox Christianity cosmology. In many ways Gnosticism may appear to be polytheistic or even pantheistic.

To understand some of the basic beliefs of Gnosticism, let us start with the common ground shared between Gnosticism and modern Christianity. Both believe the world is imperfect, corrupt, and brutal. The blame for this, according to mainstream Christianity, is placed squarely on the shoulders of man himself. With the fall of man (Adam), the world was forever changed to the undesirable and harmful place in which we live today. However, Gnostics reject this view as an incorrect interpretation of the creation myth.

According to Gnostics, the blame is not in ourselves, but in our creator. The creator of this world was himself somewhat less than perfect and in fact, deeply flawed and cruel, making mankind the child of a lesser God. It is in the book, *The Apocryphon of John*, that the Gnostic view of creation is presented to us in great detail.

Gnosticism also teaches that in the beginning a Supreme Being called The Father, The Divine All, The Origin, The Supreme God, or The Fullness, emanated the element of existence, both visible and invisible. His intent was not to create but, just as light emanates from a flame, so did creation shine forth from God. This manifested the primal element needed for creation. This was the creation of Barbelo, who is the Thought of God.

The Father's thought performed a deed and she was created from it. It is she who had appeared before him in the shining of his light. This is the first power which was before all of them and which was created from his mind. She is the Thought of the All and her light shines like his light. It is the perfect power which is the visage of the invisible. She is the pure, undefiled Spirit who is perfect. She is the first power,

The Gnostic Scriptures

the glory of Barbelo, the perfect glory of the kingdom (kingdoms), the glory revealed. She glorified the pure, undefiled Spirit and it was she who praised him, because thanks to him she had come forth.

The Apocryphon of John

It could be said that Barbelo is the creative emanation and, like the Divine All, is both male and female. It is the "agreement" of Barbelo and the Divine All, representing the union of male and female, that created the Christ Spirit and all the Aeons. In some renderings the word "Aeon" is used to designate an ethereal realm or kingdom. In other versions "Aeon" indicates the ruler of the realm. One of these rulers was called Sophia or Wisdom. Her fall began a chain of events that led to the introduction of evil into the universe.

Seeing the Divine flame of God, Sophia sought to know its origin. She sought to know the very nature of God. Sophia's passion ended in tragedy when she managed to capture a divine and creative spark, which she attempted to duplicate with her own creative force, without the union of a male counterpart. It was this act that produced the Archons, beings born outside the higher divine realm. In the development of the myth, explanations seem to point to the fact that Sophia carried the divine essence of creation from God within her but chose to attempt creation by using her own powers. It is unclear if this

11

was in an attempt to understand the Supreme God and his power, or an impetuous act that caused evil to enter the cosmos in the form of her creations.

The realm containing the Fullness of the Godhead and Sophia is called the pleroma or Realm of Fullness. This is the Gnostic heaven. The lesser Gods created in Sophia's failed attempt were cast outside the pleroma and away from the presence of God. In essence, she threw away and discarded her flawed creations.

"She cast it away from her, outside the place where no one of the immortals might see it, for she had created it in ignorance. And she surrounded it with a glowing cloud, and she put a throne in the middle of the cloud so that no one could see it except the Holy Spirit who is called the mother of all that has life. And she called his name Yaldaboth." Apocryphon of John

The beings Sophia created were imperfect and oblivious to the Supreme God. Her creations contained deities even less perfect than herself. They were called the Powers, the Rulers, or the Archons. Their leader was called the Demiurge, but his name was Yaldaboth. It was the flawed, imperfect, spiritually blind Demiurge, (Yaldaboth), who became the creator of the material world and all things in it. Gnostics considered

Yaldaboth to be the same as Jehovah (Yahweh), who is the Jewish creator God. These beings, the Demiurge and the Archons, would later equate to Satan and his demons, or Jehovah and his angels, depending on which Gnostic sect is telling the story. Both are equally evil.

In one Gnostic creation story, the Archons created Adam but could not bring him to life. In other stories Adam was formed as a type of worm, unable to attain personhood. Thus, man began as an incomplete creation of a flawed, spiritually blind, and malevolent god. In this myth, the Archons were afraid that Adam might be more powerful than the Archons themselves. When they saw Adam was incapable of attaining the human state, their fears were put to rest, thus, they called that day the "Day of Rest."

Sophia saw Adam's horrid state and had compassion, because she knew she was the origin of the Archons and their evil. Sophia descended to help bring Adam out of his hopeless condition. It is this story that set the stage for the emergence of the sacred feminine force in Gnosticism that is not seen in orthodox Christianity. Sophia brought within herself the light and power of the Supreme God. Metaphorically, within the spiritual womb of Sophia was carried the life force of the Supreme God for Adam's salvation.

In the Gnostic text called, *The Apocryphon of John*, Sophia is quoted:

> *"I entered into the midst of the cage which is the prison of the body. And I spoke saying: 'He who hears, let him awake from his deep sleep.' Then Adam wept and shed tears. After he wiped away his bitter tears he asked: 'Who calls my name, and from where has this hope arose in me even while I am in the chains of this prison?' And I (Sophia) answered: 'I am the one who carries the pure light; I am the thought of the undefiled spirit. Arise, remember, and follow your origin, which is I, and beware of the deep sleep.'"*

Sophia would later equate to the Holy Spirit as it awakened the comatose soul.

As the myth evolved, Sophia, after animating Adam, became Eve in order to assist Adam in finding the truth. She offered it to him in the form of the fruit of the tree of knowledge. To Gnostics, this was an act of deliverance.

Other stories have Sophia becoming the serpent in order to offer Adam a way to attain the truth. In either case, the apple represented the hard sought truth, which was the knowledge of good and evil, and through that knowledge Adam could become a god. Later, the serpent would become a feminine symbol of wisdom, probably owing to the connection with Sophia. Eve, being Sophia in disguise, would become the mother and sacred feminine of us all. As Gnostic theology began to coalesce, Sophia would come to be considered a force or conduit of the Holy Spirit, in part due to the fact that the Holy Spirit was also considered a feminine and creative force from the Supreme God. The Gospel of Philip echoes this theology in verse six as follows:

> *In the days when we were Hebrews we were made orphans, having only our Mother. Yet when we believed in the Messiah (and became the ones of Christ), the Mother and Father both came to us.* Gospel of Philip

As the emerging orthodox church became more and more oppressive to women, later even labeling them "occasions of sin," the Gnostics countered by raising women to equal status with men, saying Sophia was, in a sense, the handmaiden or wife of the Supreme God, making the soul of Adam her spiritual offspring.

In Gnostic cosmology the "living" world is under the control of entities called Aeons, of which Sophia is head. This means the Aeons influence or control the soul, life force, intelligence, thought, and mind. Control of the mechanical or

15

inorganic world is given to the Archons. They rule the physical aspects of systems, regulation, limits, and order in the world. Both the ineptitude and cruelty of the Archons are reflected in the chaos and pain of the material realm.

The lesser God that created the world, Yaldaboth. began his existence in a state that was both detached and remote from the Supreme God in aspects both spiritual and physical. Since Sophia had misused her creative force, which passed from the Supreme God to her, Sophia's creation, the Demiurge, Yaldaboth, contained only part of the original creative spark of the Supreme Being. He was created with an imperfect nature caused by his distance in lineage and in spirit from the Divine All or Supreme God. It is because of his imperfections and limited abilities the lesser God is also called the "Half-Maker".

The Creator God, the Demiurge, and his helpers, the Archons took the stuff of existence produced by the Supreme God and fashioned it into this material world.

Since the Demiurge (Yaldaboth) had no memory of how he came to be alive, he did not realize he was not the true creator. The Demiurge believed he somehow came to create the material world by himself. The Supreme God allowed the Demiurge and Archons to remain deceived.

The Creator God (the Demiurge) intended the material world to be perfect and eternal, but he did not have it in himself to accomplish the feat. What comes forth from a being cannot be greater than the highest part of him, can it? The world was created flawed and transitory and we are part of it. Can we escape? The Demiurge was imperfect and evil. So was the world he created. If it was the Demiurge who created man and man is called upon to escape the Demiurge and find union with the Supreme God, is this not demanding that man becomes greater than his creator? Spiritually this seems impossible, but as many children become greater than their parents, man is expected to become greater than his maker, the Demiurge. This starts with the one fact that the Demiurge denies: the existence and supremacy of the Supreme God.

Man was created with a dual nature as the product of the material world of the Demiurge with his imperfect essence, combined with the spark of God that emanated from the Supreme God through Sophia. A version of the creation story has Sophia instructing the Demiurge to breath into Adam that spiritual power he had taken from Sophia during his creation. It was the spiritual power from Sophia that brought life to Adam.

It is this divine spark in man that calls to its source, the Supreme God, and which causes a "divine discontent," that nagging feeling that keeps us questioning if this is all there is.

This spark and the feeling it gives us keeps us searching for the truth.

The Creator God sought to keep man ignorant of his defective state by keeping him enslaved to the material world. By doing so, he continued to receive man's worship and servitude. He did not wish man to recognize or gain knowledge of the true Supreme God. Since he did not know or acknowledge the Supreme God, he views any attempt to worship anything else as spiritual treason.

The opposition of forces set forth in the spiritual battle over the continued enslavement of man and man's spiritual freedom set up the duality of good and evil in Gnostic theology. There was a glaring difference between the orthodox Christian viewpoint and the Gnostic viewpoint. According to Gnostics, the creator of the material world was an evil entity and the Supreme God, who was his source, was the good entity. Christians quote John 1:1 "In the beginning was the Word, and the Word was with God, and the Word was God."

According to Gnostics, only through the realization of man's true state or through death can he escape captivity in the material realm. This means the idea of salvation does not deal with original sin or blood payment. Instead, it focuses on the idea of awakening to the fullness of the truth.

According to Gnostic theology, neither Jesus nor his death can save anyone, but the truth that he came to proclaim can allow a person to save his or her own soul. It is the truth, or realization of the lie of the material world and its God, that sets one on a course of freedom.

To escape the earthly prison and find one's way back to the pleroma (heaven) and the Supreme God, is the soteriology (salvation doctrine) and eschatology (judgment, reward, and doctrine of heaven) of Gnosticism.

The idea that personal revelation leads to salvation, may be what caused the mainline Christian church to declare Gnosticism a heresy. The church could better tolerate alternative theological views if the views did not undermine the authority of the church and its ability to control the people. Gnostic theology placed salvation in the hands of the individual through personal revelations and knowledge, excluding the need for the orthodox church and its clergy to grant salvation or absolution. This fact, along with the divergent interpretation of the creation story, which placed the creator God, Yaldaboth or Jehovah, as the enemy of mankind, was too much for the church to tolerate. Reaction was harsh. Gnosticism was declared to be a dangerous heresy.

Gnosticism may be considered polytheistic because it espoused many "levels" of Gods, beginning with an ultimate, unknowable, Supreme God and descending as he created Sophia, and Sophia created the Demiurge (Creator God); each becoming more inferior and limited.

There is a hint of pantheism in Gnostic theology due to the fact that creation occurs because of a deterioration of the Godhead and the dispersion of the creative essence, which eventually devolves into the creation of man.

In the end, there occurs a universal reconciliation as being after being realizes the existence of the Supreme God and renounces the material world and its inferior creator.

Combined with its Christian influences, the cosmology of the Gnostics may have borrowed from the Greek philosopher, Plato, as well as from Buddhism. There are disturbing parallels between the creation myth set forth by Plato and some of those recorded in Gnostic writings.

Plato lived from 427 to 347 B.C. He was the son of wealthy Athenians and a student of the philosopher, Socrates, and the mathematician, Pythagoras. Plato himself was the teacher of Aristotle.

In Plato's cosmology, the Demiurge is an artist who imposed form on materials that already existed. The raw materials were in a chaotic and random state. The physical world must have had visible form which was put together much like a puzzle is constructed. This later gave way to a philosophy which stated that all things in existence could be broken down into a small subset of geometric shapes.

In the tradition of Greek mythology, Plato's cosmology began with a creation story. The story was narrated by the philosopher Timaeus of Locris, a fictional character of Plato's making. In his account, nature is initiated by a creator deity, called the "Demiurge," a name which may be the Geek word for "craftsman" or "artisan" or, according to how one divides the word, it could also be translated as "half-maker."

The Demiurge sought to create the cosmos modeled on his understanding of the supreme and original truth. In this way he created the visible universe based on invisible truths. He set in place rules of process such as birth, growth, change, death, and dissolution. This was Plato's "Realm of Becoming." It was his Genesis. Plato stated that the internal structure of the cosmos had innate intelligence and was therefore called the World Soul. The cosmic super-structure of the Demiurge was used as the framework on which to hang or fill in the details and parts of the universe. The Demiurge then appointed his underlings to fill in the details which allowed the universe to remain in a working and balanced state. All phenomena of nature resulted from an interaction and interplay of the two forces of reason and necessity.

Plato represented reason as constituting the World Soul. The material world was a necessity in which reason acted out its will in the physical realm. The duality between the will, mind, or reason of the World Soul and the material universe and its inherent flaws set in play the duality of Plato's world and is seen reflected in the beliefs of the Gnostics.

In Plato's world, the human soul was immortal, each soul was assigned to a star. Souls that were just or good were permitted to return to their stars upon their death. Unjust souls were reincarnated to try again. Escape of the soul to the freedom of the stars and out of the cycle of reincarnation was best accomplished by following the reason and goodness of the World Soul and not the physical world, which was set in place only as a necessity to manifest the patterns of the World Soul.

Although in Plato's cosmology the Demiurge was not seen as evil, in Gnostic cosmology he was considered not only to be flawed and evil, but he was also the beginning of all evil in the material universe, having created it to reflect his own malice.

Following the path of Plato's cosmology, some Gnostics left open the possibility of reincarnation if the person had not reached the truth before his death.

In the year 13 A.D. Roman annals record the visit of an Indian king named Pandya or Porus. He came to see Caesar

Augustus carrying a letter of introduction in Greek. He was accompanied by a monk who burned himself alive in the city of Athens to prove his faith in Buddhism. The event was described by Nicolaus of Damascus as, not surprisingly, causing a great stir among the people. It is thought that this was the first transmission of Buddhist teaching to the masses.

In the second century A.D., Clement of Alexandria wrote about Buddha: "Among the Indians are those philosophers also who follow the precepts of Boutta (Buddha), whom they honour as a god on account of his extraordinary sanctity." (Clement of Alexandria, "The Stromata, or Miscellanies" Book I, Chapter XV).

"Thus philosophy, a thing of the highest utility, flourished in antiquity among the barbarians, shedding its light over the nations. And afterwards it came to Greece." (Clement of Alexandria, "The Stromata, or Miscellanies").

To clarify what "philosophy" was transmitted from India to Greece, we turn to the historians Hippolytus and Epiphanius who wrote of Scythianus, a man who had visited India around 50 A.D. They report; "He brought 'the doctrine of the Two Principles.'" According to these writers, Scythianus' pupil Terebinthus called himself a Buddha. Some scholars suggest it was he that traveled to the area of Babylon and transmitted his knowledge to Mani, who later founded Manichaeism.

Adding to the possibility of Eastern influence, we have accounts of the Apostle Thomas' attempt to convert the people of Asia-Minor. If the Gnostic gospel bearing his name was truly written by Thomas, it was penned after his return from India, where he also encountered the Buddhist influences.

Ancient church historians mention that Thomas preached to the Parthians in Persia, and it is said he was buried in Edessa. Fourth century chronicles attribute the evangelization of India (Asia-Minor or Central Asia) to Thomas.

The texts of the Gospel of Thomas, which some believe predate the four gospels, has a very "Zen-like" or Eastern flavor.

Since it is widely held that the four gospels of Matthew, Mark, Luke, and John have a common reference in the basic text of Mark, it stands to reason that all follow the same general insight and language. If The Gospel of Thomas was written in his absence from the other apostles or if it was the first gospel written, one can assume it was written outside the influences common to the other gospels.

Although the codex found in Egypt is dated to the fourth century, the actual construction of the text of Thomas is placed by most Biblical scholars at about 70–150 A.D. Most agree the time of writing was in the second century A.D.

Following the transmission of the philosophy of "Two Principals," both Manichaeism and Gnosticism retained a dualistic viewpoint. The black-versus-white dualism of Gnosticism came to rest in the evil of the material world and its maker, versus the goodness of the freed soul and the Supreme God with whom it seeks union.

Oddly, the disdain for the material world and its Creator God drove Gnostic theology to far-flung extremes in attitude, beliefs, and actions. Gnostics idolize the serpent in the "Garden of Eden" story. After all, if your salvation hinges on secret knowledge the offer of becoming gods through the knowledge of good and evil sounds wonderful. So powerful was the draw of this "knowledge myth" to the Gnostics that the serpent became linked to Sophia by some sects. This can still be seen today in our medical and veterinarian symbols of serpents on poles, conveying the ancient meanings of knowledge and wisdom.

Genesis 3 (King James Version)

1 Now the serpent was more subtil than any beast of the field which the LORD God had made. And he said unto the woman, Yea, hath God said, Ye shall not eat of every tree of the garden?

2 And the woman said unto the serpent, We may eat of the fruit of the trees of the garden:

3 But of the fruit of the tree which is in the midst of the garden, God hath said, Ye shall not eat of it, neither shall ye touch it, lest ye die.

4 And the serpent said unto the woman, Ye shall not surely die:

5 For God doth know that in the day ye eat thereof, then your eyes shall be opened, and ye shall be as Gods, knowing good and evil.

It is because of their vehement struggle against the Creator God and the search for some transcendent truth, that Gnostics held the people of Sodom in high regard. The people of Sodom sought to "corrupt" the messengers sent by their enemy, the Creator God. Anything done to thwart the Demiurge and his minions was considered valiant.

Genesis 19 (King James Version)

1 And there came two angels to Sodom at even; and Lot sat in the gate of Sodom: and Lot seeing them rose up to meet them; and he bowed himself with his face toward the ground;

2 And he said, Behold now, my lords, turn in, I pray you, into your servant's house, and tarry all night, and wash your feet, and ye shall rise up early, and go on your ways. And they said, Nay; but we will abide in the street all night.

3 And he pressed upon them greatly; and they turned in unto him, and entered into his house; and he made them a feast, and did bake unleavened bread, and they did eat.

4 But before they lay down, the men of the city, even the men of Sodom, compassed the house round, both old and young, all the people from every quarter:

5 And they called unto Lot, and said unto him, Where are the men which came in to thee this night? bring them out unto us, that we may know them.

6 And Lot went out at the door unto them, and shut the door after him,

7 And said, I pray you, brethren, do not so wickedly.

8 Behold now, I have two daughters which have not known man; let me, I pray you, bring them out unto you, and do ye to them as is good in your eyes: only unto these men do nothing; for therefore came they under the shadow of my roof.

9 And they said, Stand back. And they said again, This one fellow came in to sojourn, and he will needs be a judge: now will we deal worse with thee, than with them. And they pressed sore upon the man, even Lot, and came near to break the door.

10 But the men put forth their hand, and pulled Lot into the house to them, and shut to the door.

To modern Christians, the idea of admiring the serpent, which we believe was Satan, may seem unthinkable. Supporting the idea of attacking and molesting the angels sent to Sodom to warn of the coming destruction seems appalling; but to Gnostics the real evil was the malevolent entity, the Creator God of this world. To destroy his messengers, as was the case in Sodom, would impede his mission. To obtain knowledge of good and evil, as was offered by the serpent in the garden, would set the captives free.

To awaken the inner knowledge of the true God was the battle. The material world was designed to prevent the awakening by entrapping, confusing, and distracting the spirit of man. The aim of Gnosticism was the spiritual awakening and freedom of man.

Gnostics, in the age of the early church, would preach to converts (novices) about this awakening, saying the novice must awaken the God within himself and see the trap that was the material world. Salvation came from the recognition or knowledge contained in this spiritual awakening.

Not all people are ready or willing to accept the Gnosis. Many are bound to the material world and are satisfied to be only as and where they are. These have mistaken the Creator God for the Supreme God and do not know there is anything beyond the Creator God or the material existence. These people know only the lower or earthly wisdom and not the higher wisdom above the Creator God. They are referred to as "dead."

Gnostic sects split primarily into two categories. Both branches held that those who were truly enlightened could no longer be influenced by the material world. Both divisions of Gnosticism believed that their spiritual journey could not be impeded by the material realm since the two were not only separate but in opposition. Such an attitude influenced some Gnostics toward Stoicism, choosing to abstain from the world, and others toward Epicureanism, choosing to indulge.

Major schools fell into two categories; those who rejected the material world of the Creator God, and those who rejected the laws of the Creator God. For those who rejected the world the Creator God had spawned, overcoming the material world was accomplished by partaking of as little of the world and its pleasures as possible. These followers lived very stark and ascetic lives, abstaining from meat, sex, marriage, and all things that would entice them to remain in the material realm.

Other schools believed it was their duty to simply defy the Creator God and all laws that he had proclaimed. Since the Creator God had been identified as Jehovah, God of the Jews, these followers set about to break every law held dear by Christians and Jews.

As human nature is predisposed to do, many Gnostics took up the more wanton practices, believing that nothing done in their earthly bodies would affect their spiritual lives. Whether it was excesses in sex, alcohol, food, or any other assorted debaucheries, the Gnostics were safe within their faith, believing nothing spiritually bad could come of their earthly adventures.

The actions of the Gnostics are mentioned by early Church leaders. One infamous Gnostic school is actually mentioned in the Bible, as we will read later.

The world was out of balance, inferior, and corrupt. The spirit was perfect and intact. It was up to the Gnostics to tell the story, explain the error, and awaken the world to the light of truth. The Supreme God had provided a vehicle to help in their effort. He had created a teacher of light and truth.

Since the time of Sophia's mistaken creation of the Archons, there was an imbalance in the cosmos. The Supreme God began to re-establish the balance by producing Christ to teach and save man. That left only Sophia, now in a fallen and bound state, along with the Demiurge, and the Archons to upset the cosmic equation. In this theology one might loosely equate the Supreme God to the New Testament Christian God,

Demiurge to Satan, the Archons to demons, the pleroma to heaven, and Sophia to the creative or regenerative force of the Holy Spirit. This holds up well except for one huge problem. If the Jews believed that Jehovah created all things, and the Gnostic believed that the Demiurge created all things, then to the Gnostic mind, the Demiurge must be Old Testament god, Jehovah, and that made Jehovah their enemy.

For those who seek that which is beyond the material world and its flawed creator, the Supreme God has sent Messengers of Light to awaken the divine spark of the Supreme God within us. This part of us will call to the True God as deep calls to deep. The greatest and most perfect Messenger of Light was the Christ. He is also referred to as The Good, Christ, Messiah, and The Word. He came to reveal the Divine Light to us in the form of knowledge.

According to the Gnostics, Christ came to show us our own divine spark and to awaken us to the illusion of the material world and its flawed maker. He came to show us the way back to the divine Fullness (The Supreme God). The path to enlightenment was the knowledge sleeping within each of us. Christ came to show us the Christ spirit living in each of us. Individual ignorance or the refusal to awaken our internal divine spark was the only original sin. Christ was the only Word spoken by God that could awaken us. Christ was also the embodiment of the Word itself. He was part of the original transmission from the Supreme God that took form on the earth to awaken the soul of man so that man might search beyond the material world.

One Gnostic view of the Incarnation was "docetic," which is an early heretical position that Jesus was never actually present in the flesh, but only appeared to be human. He was a spiritual being and his human appearance was only an illusion. Of course, the title of "heretical" can only be decided by the controlling authority of the time. In this case it was the church that was about to emerge under the rule of the Emperor Constantine.

Most Gnostics held that the Christ spirit indwelt the earthly Jesus at the time of his baptism by John, at which time Jesus received the name, and thus the power, of the Lord or Supreme God.

The Christ spirit departed from Jesus' body before his death. These two viewpoints remove the idea of God sacrificing himself as an atonement for the sins of man. The idea of atonement was not necessary in Gnostic theology since it was knowledge and not sacrifice that set one free.

Since there was a distinction in Gnosticism between the man Jesus and the Light of Christ that came to reside within him, it is not contrary to Gnostic beliefs that Mary Magdalene could have been the consort and wife of Jesus. Neither would it have been blasphemous for them to have had children.

Various sects of Gnosticism stressed certain elements of their basic theology. Each had its head teachers and its special flavor of beliefs. One of the oldest types was the Syrian Gnosticism. It existed around 120 A.D. In contrast to other sects, the Syrian lacked much of the embellished mythology of Aeons, Archons, and angels.

The fight between the Supreme God and the Creator God was not eternal, though there was strong opposition to Jehovah, the Creator God. He was considered to have been the last of the seven angels who created this world out of divine material which emanated from the Supreme God. The Demiurge attempted to create man, but only created a miserable worm which the Supreme God had to save by giving it the spark of divine life. Thus man was born.

According to this sect, Jehovah, the Creator God, must not be worshiped. The Supreme God calls us to his service and presence through Christ his Son. They pursued only the unknowable Supreme God and sought to obey the Supreme Deity by abstaining from eating meat and from marriage and sex, and by leading an ascetic life. The symbol of Christ was the serpent, who attempted to free Adam and Eve from their ignorance and entrapment to the Creator God.

Another Gnostic school was the Hellenistic or Alexandrian School. These systems absorbed the philosophy and concepts of the Greeks, and the Semitic nomenclature was replaced by Greek names. The cosmology and myth had grown out of proportion and appear to our eyes to be unwieldy. Yet, this school produced two great thinkers, Basilides and Valentinus. Though born at Antioch, in Syria, Basilides founded his school in Alexandria around the year A.D. 130, where it survived for several centuries.

Valentinus first taught at Alexandria and then in Rome. He established the largest Gnostic movement around A.D. 160. This movement was founded on an elaborate mythology and a system of sexual duality of male and female interplay, both in its deities and its savior.

Tertullian wrote that between 135 A.D. and 160 A.D. Valentinus, a prominent Gnostic, had great influence in the Christian church. Valentinus ascended in church hierarchy and became a candidate for the office of bishop of Rome, the office that quickly evolved into that of Pope. He lost the election by a narrow margin. Even though Valentinus was outspoken about his Gnostic slant on Christianity, he was a respected member of the Christian community until his death and was probably a practicing bishop in a church of lesser status than the one in Rome.

The main platform of Gnosticism was the ability to transcend the material world through the possession of privileged and directly imparted knowledge. Following this doctrine, Valentinus claimed to have been instructed by a direct disciple of one of Jesus' apostles, a man by the name of Theodas.

Valentinus is considered by many to be the father of modern Gnosticism. His vision of the faith is summarized by G.R.S. Mead in the book "Fragments of a Faith Forgotten."

> "The Gnosis in his hands is trying to embrace everything, even the most dogmatic formulation of the traditions of the Master. The great popular movement and its incomprehensibilities were recognized by Valentinus as an integral part of the mighty outpouring; he laboured to weave all together, external and internal, into one piece, devoted his life to the task, and doubtless only at his death perceived that for that age he was attempting the impossible. None but the very few could ever appreciate the ideal of the man, much less understand it. " (Fragments of a Faith Forgotten, p. 297)

Gnostic theology seemed to vacillate from polytheism to pantheism to dualism to monotheism, depending on the teacher and how he viewed and stressed certain areas of their creation myths. Marcion, a Gnostic teacher, espoused differences between the God of the New Testament and the God of the Old Testament, claiming they were two separate entities. According to Marcion, the New Testament God was a good true God while the Old Testament God was an evil angel. Although this may be a heresy, it pulled his school back into monotheism. The church, however, disowned him.

Syneros and Prepon, disciples of Marcion, postulated three different entities, carrying their teachings from monotheism into polytheism in one stroke. In their system the opponent of the good God was not the God of the Jews, but Eternal Matter, which was the source of all evil. Matter, in this system became a principal creative force. Although it was created imperfect, it could also create, having the innate intelligence of the "world soul."

Of all the Gnostic schools or sects the most famous is the Antinomian School. Believing that the Creator God, Jehovah, was evil, they sat out to disrupt all things connected to the Jewish God. This included his laws. It was considered their duty to break any law of morality, diet, or conduct given by the Jewish God, who they considered the evil Creator God. The leader of the sect was called Nicolaites. The sect existed in Apostolic times and is mentioned in the Bible.

Revelation 2 (King James Version)

5 Remember therefore from whence thou art fallen, and repent, and do the first works; or else I will come unto thee quickly, and will remove thy candlestick out of his place, except thou repent.

6 But this thou hast, that thou hatest the deeds of the Nicolaitanes, which I also hate.

Revelation 2 (King James Version)

14 But I have a few things against thee, because thou hast there them that hold the doctrine of Balaam, who taught Balac to cast a stumbling block before the children of Israel, to eat things sacrificed unto idols, and to commit fornication.

15 So hast thou also them that hold the doctrine of the Nicolaitanes, which thing I hate.

16 Repent; or else I will come unto thee quickly, and will fight against them with the sword of my mouth.

One of the leaders of the Nocolaitanes, according to Origen, was Carpocrates, whom Tertullian called a magician and a fornicator. Carpocretes taught that one could only escape the cosmic powers by discharging one's obligations to them and disregarding their laws. The Christian church fathers, St. Justin, Irenaeus, and Eusebius wrote that the reputation of these men (the Nicolaitanes), brought infamy upon the whole race of Christians.

Although Gnostic sects varied, they had certain points in common. These commonalities included salvation through special knowledge, and the fact that the world was corrupt as it was created by an evil God.

According to Gnostic theology, nothing can come from the material world that is not flawed. Because of this, Gnostics did not believe that Christ could have been a corporeal being. Thus, there must be some separation or distinction between Jesus, as a man, and Christ, as a spiritual being born from the Supreme, unrevealed, and eternal God.

To closer examine this theology, we turn to Valentinus, the driving force of early Gnosticism, for an explanation. Valentinus divided Jesus Christ into two very distinct parts; Jesus, the man, and Christ, the anointed spiritual messenger of God. These two forces met in the moment of Baptism when the Spirit of God came to rest on Jesus and the Christ power entered his body.

Here Gnosticism runs aground on its own theology, for if the spiritual cannot mingle with the material then how can the Christ spirit inhabit a body? The result of the dichotomy was a schism within Gnosticism. Some held to the belief that the specter of Jesus was simply an illusion produced by Christ himself to enable him to do his work on earth. It was not real, not matter, not corporeal, and did not actually exist as a physical body would. Others came to believe that Jesus must have been a specially prepared vessel and was the perfect human body formed by the very essence of the plumora (heaven). It was this path of thought that allowed Jesus to continue as human, lover, and father.

Jesus, the man, became a vessel containing the Light of God, called Christ. In the Gnostic view we all could and should become Christs, carrying the Truth and Light of God. We are all potential vehicles of the same Spirit that Jesus held within him when he was awakened to the Truth.

The suffering and death of Jesus then took on much less importance in the Gnostic view, as Jesus was simply part of the corrupt world and was suffering the indignities of this world as any man would. Therefore, from their viewpoint, he could have been married and been a father without disturbing Gnostic theology in the least.

The Gnostic texts seem to divide man into parts, although at times the divisions are somewhat unclear. The divisions alluded to may include the soul, which is the will of man; the spirit, which is depicted as wind or air (pneuma) and contains the holy spark that is the spirit of God in man; and the material human form, the body. The mind of man sits as a mediator between the soul, or will, and the spirit, which is connected to God.

Without the light of the truth, the spirit is held captive by the Demiurge, which enslaves man. This entrapment is called "sickness." It is this sickness that the Light came to heal and then to set us free. The third part of man, his material form, was considered a weight, an anchor, and a hindrance, keeping man attached to the corrupted earthly realm.

As we read the text, we must realize that Gnosticism conflicted with traditional Christianity. Overall theology can rise and fall upon small words and terms. If Jesus was not God, his death and thus his atonement meant nothing. His suffering meant nothing. Even the resurrection meant nothing, if one's view of Jesus was that he was not human to begin with, as was true with some Gnostics.

For the Gnostics, resurrection of the dead was unthinkable since flesh as well as all matter is destined to perish. According to Gnostic theology, there was no resurrection of the flesh, but only of the soul. How the soul would be resurrected was explained differently by various Gnostic groups, but all denied the resurrection of the body. To the enlightened Gnostic the actual person was the spirit who used the body as an instrument to survive in the material world but did not identify with it. This belief is echoed in the Gospel of Thomas.

> *29. Jesus said: If the flesh came into being because of spirit, it is a marvel, but if spirit came into being because of the body, it would be a marvel of marvels. I marvel indeed at how great wealth has taken up residence in this poverty.*

Owing to the Gnostic belief of such a separation of spirit and body, it was thought that the Christ spirit within the body of Jesus departed the body before the crucifixion. Others said the body was an illusion and the crucifixion was a sham perpetrated by an eternal spirit on the men that sought to kill it. Lastly, some suggested that Jesus deceived the soldiers into thinking he was dead. The resurrection under this circumstance became a lie which allowed Jesus to escape and live on in anonymity, hiding, living as a married man, and raising a family until his natural death.

Think of the implications to the orthodox Christian world if the spirit of God departed from Jesus as it fled and laughed as the body was crucified. This is the implication of the Gnostic interpretation of the death of Jesus when he cries out, "My power, my power, why have you left me," as the Christ spirit left his body before his death. What are the ramifications to the modern Christian if the Creator God, the Demiurge, is more evil than his creation? Can a Creation rise above its creator? Is it possible for man to find the spark within himself that calls to the Supreme God and free himself of his evil creator?

Although, in time, the creation myth and other Gnostic differences began to be swept under the rug, it was the division between Jesus and the Christ spirit that put them at odds with the emerging orthodox church. At the establishment of the doctrine of the trinity, the mainline church firmly set a divide between themselves and the Gnostics.

To this day there is a battle raging in the Christian world as believers and seekers attempt to reconcile today's Christianity to the sect of the early Christian church called, "Gnosticism."

The Sacred Feminine

One of the most striking differences between the Gnostic church and the modern church is the absence of reverence for Mary, the mother of Jesus. This is due in part to the fact that today's accepted traditions of Mother Mary were not yet in place. In fact, some of the positions of the Catholic Church regarding Mary were not officially accepted until the mid to late nineteenth century.

In the writings of the early church fathers (Justin Martyr 165 A.D. and Irenaeus 202 A.D.), Mother Mary was seldom mentioned and only to contrast Mary's obedience with Eve's disobedience. The doctrine of Mary as Theotokos (God-bearer) probably originated in Alexandria and was first introduced by Origen. It became common in the fourth century and accepted at the Council of Ephesus in 431 A.D.

Since the orthodox Christian church continued to slip farther and farther toward the belief that sex was evil, the doctrine of the "Ever-Virginity" of Mary was established. This was the belief that Mary conceived as a virgin, but also remained a virgin even after giving birth to Jesus and thereafter for the rest of her life. The Catholic Church rejects the idea that Mary had other children, although the Bible speaks of the

43

brothers and sisters of Jesus. The doctrine of "virginity" was established around 359 A.D.

The doctrine of the bodily Assumption of Mary was formally developed by St. Gregory of Tours around 594 A.D. This doctrine stated that Mary, the mother of Jesus, was taken up into heaven to be seated at the side of Jesus. The idea has been present in apocryphal texts since the late fourth century.

The Feast of the Assumption became widespread in the sixth century, and sermons on that occasion tended to emphasize Mary's power in heaven.

Of all the doctrines regarding Mary, the doctrine of the Immaculate Conception widened the divide between the Catholic churches and other Christian churches. This doctrine took the position that Mother Mary was born without the stain of original sin. Both Catholics and Orthodox Christians accept this doctrine, but only the Roman Catholic Church has named it "The Immaculate Conception" and articulated it as doctrine.

Eastern Orthodox Christians reject the western doctrine of original sin, preferring instead to speak of a tendency towards sin. They believe Mary was born without sin, but so was everyone else. Mary simply never gave in to sin.

As we see in the following statement, the doctrine was not formally accepted until 1854 A.D.

"The Most Blessed Virgin Mary was, from the first moment of her conception, by a singular grace and privilege of almighty God and by virtue of the merits of Jesus Christ, Savior of the human race, preserved immune from all stain of original sin."
Pope Pius IX, Ineffabilis Deus (1854)

The evolution of the status of Mary the Mother of Jesus has taken eighteen-hundred years to become what it is today. The status of Mary Magdalene was likely established within the Gnostic communities by 400 A.D.

Gnostic texts often used sex as a metaphor for spiritual union and release. Since the Godhead itself had both a masculine element of the Supreme God, who is the Father, and a feminine element of Sophia, sexual terms are used freely. The sexual metaphor was expanded in the story of the Supreme God giving rise to Sophia as he spewed forth the essence of everything. According to some sects Sophia became the creator or divine mother of both angels and lesser Gods, including the creator of the material world, the Demiurge.

Sexual duality found in Gnosticism, along with the concept of the sacred feminine seen in the Sophia myth, allowed for more reverence and acceptance of women in the Gnostic worship. Owing to this, the concept that Mary Magdalene was somehow special to Jesus, as is reported in the *Gospel of Philip*, or that he may have shared spiritual concepts with her that were unknown to the male apostles, as told in the *Gospel of Mary Magdalene*, is not so difficult to comprehend.

The parallel between Sophia and Mary Magdalene cannot be overstated. Sophia was the handmaiden of the Supreme God, carrying the life force, which was the emanation of God. She carried the truth within her, which she offered to Adam. The truth was offered up to set him free. Mary was the consort of Jesus, carrying the imparted knowledge and possibly his life force in the form of a child. She revealed to the apostles the truth Jesus personally and intimately gave to her alone. We will see this stated clearly in *The Gospel of Mary Magdalene* later in this book.

The mythos of Gnosticism's sacred feminine force comes full circle in the person of Mary Magdalene. From God to Sophia; from Sophia to the man Adam; from the second Adam, who is Christ Jesus, to Mary Magdalene, who offered up that which was given her to mankind; the circle of knowledge and life was complete once again.

Points of Logic, Faith, and Sex

Man's inability to understand the divine is eclipsed only by his inadequacy to accurately articulate what his feeble mind has so tenuously grasped. Each time man desires to "tinker" with theology in order to make that which is spiritual reasonable and logical to the carnal mind, more problems are raised than solved.

When the Gnostics began to entertain the idea of the man Jesus being the vessel and host of the Holy Spirit they broke from their first basic tenet of faith: that which states that the spiritual world could not co-mingled, with the material world. As Gnostic theology developed, lines blurred and softened to a point where it was realized that if man was a triune being of body, soul, and spirit there must be a level of interface between the two worlds. At this point it was decided that only the Supreme God was too holy and pure to interact with the material world. This left open the possibility for the man Jesus to carry the Holy Spirit.

But wait... isn't God and the Holy Spirit the same? They must not be for this belief to work. If they were the same then the symbiotic relationship of Jesus the man and the Holy Spirit of the Supreme God would not have allowed itself to have a relationship with Mary Magdalene.

Even though Jesus was considered the highest earthly creation, he was still not the equal of God.

Yet, according to theology being proclaimed by the established churches, the Holy Spirit was not only equal to God but the essentially the same as God. This presented a point of illogic in the Gnostic theology. This was solved by some Gnostic slight of hand. Since the Holy Spirit was a feminine force, it was not actually God, but was the spouse of the Supreme God. This set the stage for further parallels between Sophia and the Holy Spirit.

Rising to another level of the Sacred Feminine, it becomes the female part of the Godhead that empowered Jesus. The mother of the Godhead becomes the Christ Spirit that saves and leads mankind.

Later, as the Catholic Church struggled to make sense of their own female redeemer, they began to elevate Mother Mary by announcing the doctrine of the Immaculate Conception, so errors in logic were exposed. If Mother Mary was conceived without sin in order to carry Jesus, who was conceived without sin, one must ask why it wasn't necessary for the mother of Mary to also be conceived without sin. This logic continues backward ad infinitum until Eve herself and all female offspring must be sinless. Of course, the church flatly refuses this line of reasoning, saying only that certain things must be taken on faith. This is the same tact taken regarding the "Ever-Virginity" of Mother Mary, even in the face of scriptures proclaiming that the mother, sister, and brothers of Jesus had come to have audience with him.

It was the Greek Orthodox church that already had the answer to this dilemma. Original sin is not in their doctrine. They state only that humans are born with a predisposition toward sinning. This makes null the problem of sinless birth from the beginning.

Even though the theological events of doctrine concerning Mother Mary occurred over time, they serve as an undeniable pattern of the Catholic Church as it endeavored to "purify" women and rid them of sexuality.

It was the Gnostics that continued to increase the sexuality, power, and place of women in the schema of their faith.

The sexual metaphors used in the Gnostic texts have fanned the flames of great controversy and speculation. It has been widely accepted that societal norms of the time dictated that Jewish men were to be married by the age of thirty. This certainly applied to Rabbis, since marriage and procreation were considered divine commands. Jesus is referred to by the title of Rabbi in the Bible. It has been noted that his marital status would have placed him into a very small minority in the culture at the time, being a male over 30 years of age and unmarried. Thus, some Gnostic followers use this observation to bolster the idea Jesus was married. This idea was held by those who thought that Jesus, the man, was the vehicle for the Christ spirit.

For other Gnostics who believed Jesus to be an illusion placed on us by the Christ spirit while he was on earth, the idea of a spiritual illusion mingling with flesh was out of the question.

Most Gnostics held to the idea of the duality of sexes playing out in multiple layers. The feminine force of Sophia becomes the feminine force of the Holy Spirit and is made the bride of God. The sexual duality continues when the feminine force of the Holy Spirit inhabits the perfect man, Jesus, making him the messiah. The sexual context is ripe for the story to be continued in the persons of Jesus and Mary Magdalene, physically shadowing the spiritual relationship of the Holy Spirit and the Supreme God as well as Jesus and the Holy Spirit.

The concept of a married Jesus is revealed in several verses of The Gospel of Philip such verse 118.

There is the Son of Man and there is the son of the son of Man.
The Lord is the Son of Man, and his son creates through him.
God gave the Son of Man the power to create; he also gave him
the ability to have children.   Gospel of Philip

If one were to examine the writings of Solomon, the play on words between the sexual and the spiritual aspects can be seen clearly. The Gnostics simply expanded on the theme.

Song of Solomon 1 (King James Version)
1 The song of songs, which is Solomon's.
2 Let him kiss me with the kisses of his mouth: for thy love is better than wine.
3 Because of the savour of thy good ointments thy name is as ointment poured forth, therefore do the virgins love thee.
4 Draw me, we will run after thee: the king hath brought me into his chambers: we will be glad and rejoice in thee, we will remember thy love more than wine:

Song of Solomon 2
16 My beloved is mine, and I am his: he feedeth among the lilies.
17 Until the day break, and the shadows flee away, turn, my beloved, and be thou like a roe or a young hart upon the mountains of Bether.

Song of Solomon 3

1 By night on my bed I sought him whom my soul loveth: I sought him, but I found him not.

2 I will rise now, and go about the city in the streets, and in the broad ways I will seek him whom my soul loveth: I sought him, but I found him not...

Song of Solomon 5

1 I am come into my garden, my sister, my spouse: I have gathered my myrrh with my spice; I have eaten my honeycomb with my honey; I have drunk my wine with my milk: eat, O friends; drink, yea, drink abundantly, O beloved.

2 I sleep, but my heart waketh: it is the voice of my beloved that knocketh, saying, Open to me, my sister, my love, my dove, my undefiled: for my head is filled with dew, and my locks with the drops of the night.

3 I have put off my coat; how shall I put it on? I have washed my feet; how shall I defile them?

4 My beloved put in his hand by the hole of the door, and my bowels were moved for him.

5 I rose up to open to my beloved; and my hands dropped with myrrh, and my fingers with sweet smelling myrrh, upon the handles of the lock.

Song of Solomon 7

1 How beautiful are thy feet with shoes, O prince's daughter! the joints of thy thighs are like jewels, the work of the hands of a cunning workman.

2 Thy navel is like a round goblet, which wanteth not liquor: thy belly is like an heap of wheat set about with lilies.

3 Thy two breasts are like two young roes that are twins.

Due to the inherent dualism of Gnosticism, sex was a symbol, and, at times, a portal to a mystical experience. Many religions are replete with sexual allegories, as is Gnosticism. Proceeding from the two points of sexual metaphor in Gnostic literature and the likelihood of marriage among the population of Jewish men, controversy arose when speculation began as to whether Jesus could have married. The flames of argument roared into inferno proportions when the translation of the books of Philip and Mary Magdalene were published.

And the companion (Consort) was Mary of Magdala (Mary Magdalene). The Lord loved Mary more than all the other disciples and he kissed her often on her mouth (the text is missing here and the word "mouth" is assumed). The others saw his love for Mary and asked him: "Why do you love her more than all of us?" The Savior replied, "Why do I not love you in the same way I love her?"

  The Gospel of Philip

Peter said to Mary; "Sister we know that the Savior loved you more than all other women. Tell us the words of the Savior that you remember and know, but we have not heard and do not know. Mary answered him and said; "I will tell you what He hid from you."

  The Gospel of Mary Magdalene

Seizing on the texts above, writers of both fiction and non-fiction allowed their pens to run freely amidst conjecture and speculation of marriage and children between Jesus and Mary Magdalene.

The writers *of The Da Vinci Code* and *Holy Blood, Holy Grail* took these passages and expanded them into storylines that have held readers captive with anticipation.

Did Jesus take Mary to be his wife? Could the couple have produced children? Gnostic theology leaves open the possibility.

As we step into the Gospel of Philip we encounter pure Gnostic ritual. The most sacred of all Gnostic rituals is contained in the metaphor of the duality of man and God seeking unity. With this in mind, the Lord established five sacraments: baptism, anointing, the Eucharist, redemption, and the Bridal-Chamber.

Whether the sacrament of the Bridal-Chamber was a ritual enacted by a man and woman, or strictly an allegory we may never know. All we know is that the concept of the Bridal-Chamber, where two become one, dualities merge into unity, and man finally unites with the truth within himself and finds the Supreme God is a recurring and central theme and experience of Gnosticism. Accordingly, the Gnostic Jesus would have likely been married as he led others by example.

Why, out of all the women in his life and travels, did he choose Mary of Magdala? Who was she? What made her special? Let us examine the evidence.

Who Was Mary Magdalene?

The Gospel of Philip shines light on a special connection between Jesus and Mary Magdalene. Philip calls Mary the Lord's "companion," a word that can mean "wife." But, who was this Mary, the Magdalene?

As was customary in Biblical times, the last name of the person was connected to his or her place of ancestry. This is evidenced in the fact that Jesus was called, "Jesus of Nazareth." Mary came from a town called Magdala, which was 120 miles north of Jerusalem on the shores of the Sea of Galilee. Magdala Tarichaea may have been the full name of the town. Magdala means tower, and Tarichaea means salted fish. The little village had the optimistic name of "The Tower of Salted Fish." The main business of the area was fishing, and there is a good chance that Mary worked in the fish markets, or actually owned a business selling fish. Magdala, it seems, was a prosperous fishing village with a reputation as a licentious city. Mary Magdalene apparently had money since Luke says that she ministered to Jesus out of her "substance."

The Jewish text, "Lamentations Raba," mentions a town called "Magdala," and says Magdala was judged by God and destroyed because of its fornication. This could explain western

Christianity's assumption that Mary Magdalene was the prostitute caught in adultery and presented to Jesus.

In fact, we have linked Mary Magdalene with many of the women in the New Testament who were redeemed or forgiven. This is a powerful and rich myth that resonates with both men and women who have fallen from grace and seek redemption. However, the Bible never says that Mary Magdalene was ever a prostitute.

Luke does not name her as the woman who washes the feet of Jesus with her hair.

Luke 7 (King James Version)

36 And one of the Pharisees desired him that he would eat with him. And he went into the Pharisee's house, and sat down to meat.

37 And, behold, a woman in the city, which was a sinner, when she knew that Jesus sat at meat in the Pharisee's house, brought an alabaster box of ointment,

38 And stood at his feet behind him weeping, and began to wash his feet with tears, and did wipe them with the hairs of her head, and kissed his feet, and anointed them with the ointment.

39 Now when the Pharisee which had bidden him saw it, he spake within himself, saying, This man, if he were a prophet, would have known who and what manner of woman this is that toucheth him: for she is a sinner.

57

40 *And Jesus answering said unto him, Simon, I have somewhat to say unto thee. And he saith, Master, say on.*

41 *There was a certain creditor which had two debtors: the one owed five hundred pence, and the other fifty.*

42 *And when they had nothing to pay, he frankly forgave them both. Tell me therefore, which of them will love him most?*

43 *Simon answered and said, I suppose that he, to whom he forgave most. And he said unto him, Thou hast rightly judged.*

44 *And he turned to the woman, and said unto Simon, Seest thou this woman? I entered into thine house, thou gavest me no water for my feet: but she hath washed my feet with tears, and wiped them with the hairs of her head.*

45 *Thou gavest me no kiss: but this woman since the time I came in hath not ceased to kiss my feet.*

46 *My head with oil thou didst not anoint: but this woman hath anointed my feet with ointment.*

47 *Wherefore I say unto thee, Her sins, which are many, are forgiven; for she loved much: but to whom little is forgiven, the same loveth little.*

48 *And he said unto her, Thy sins are forgiven.*

49 *And they that sat at meat with him began to say within themselves, Who is this that forgiveth sins also?*

50 *And he said to the woman, Thy faith hath saved thee; go in peace.*

There is never a name given to the woman caught in the act of adultery.

John 8 (King James Version)

1Jesus went unto the mount of Olives.

2And early in the morning he came again into the temple, and all the people came unto him; and he sat down, and taught them.

3And the scribes and Pharisees brought unto him a woman taken in adultery; and when they had set her in the midst,

4They say unto him, Master, this woman was taken in adultery, in the very act.

5Now Moses in the law commanded us, that such should be stoned: but what sayest thou?

6This they said, tempting him, that they might have to accuse him. But Jesus stooped down, and with his finger wrote on the ground, as though he heard them not.

7So when they continued asking him, he lifted up himself, and said unto them, He that is without sin among you, let him first cast a stone at her.

8And again he stooped down, and wrote on the ground.

9And they which heard it, being convicted by their own conscience, went out one by one, beginning at the eldest, even unto the last: and Jesus was left alone, and the woman standing in the midst.

10*When Jesus had lifted up himself, and saw none but the woman, he said unto her, Woman, where are those thine accusers? hath no man condemned thee?*

11*She said, No man, Lord. And Jesus said unto her, Neither do I condemn thee: go, and sin no more.*

12*Then spake Jesus again unto them, saying, I am the light of the world: he that followeth me shall not walk in darkness, but shall have the light of life.*

The only clear history we have is a single statement that it was Mary who was once demon-possessed.

Luke 8 (King James Version)

1*And it came to pass afterward, that he went throughout every city and village, preaching and shewing the glad tidings of the kingdom of God: and the twelve were with him,*

2*And certain women, which had been healed of evil spirits and infirmities, Mary called Magdalene, out of whom went seven devils,*

3*And Joanna the wife of Chuza Herod's steward, and Susanna, and many others, which ministered unto him of their substance.*

Here is what we know with certainty:

She was a woman who followed Jesus as he ministered and preached.

Luke 8:1-3: Afterward, Jesus journeyed from one town and village to another, preaching and proclaiming the good news of the kingdom of God. Accompanying him were the Twelve and some women who had been cured of evil spirits and infirmities, Mary, called Magdalene, from whom seven demons had gone out, Joanna, the wife of Herod's steward Chuza, Susanna, and many others who provided for them out of their resources.

She was there when Jesus was crucified.

Mark 15:40: There were also some women looking on from a distance, among whom were Mary Magdalene, and Mary the mother of James the Less and Joses, and Salome.
Matthew 27:56: Among them was Mary Magdalene, and Mary the mother of James and Joseph, and the mother of the sons of Zebedee.

John 19:25: But standing by the cross of Jesus were His mother, and His mother's sister, Mary the wife of Clopas, and Mary Magdalene.

She continued to believe in Jesus after he was killed.

Mark 15:47: Mary Magdalene and Mary the mother of Joses were looking on to see where He was laid.

Matthew 27:61: And Mary Magdalene was there, and the other Mary, sitting opposite the grave.

Matthew 28:1: Now after the Sabbath, as it began to dawn toward the first day of the week, Mary Magdalene and the other Mary came to look at the grave.

Mark 16:1: When the Sabbath was over, Mary Magdalene, and Mary the mother of James, and Salome, bought spices, so that they might come and anoint Him.

She was the first to realize and announce the resurrection of Jesus.

John 20:1: Now on the first day of the week Mary Magdalene came early to the tomb, while it was still dark, and saw the stone already taken away from the tomb.

Mark 16:9: Now after He had risen early on the first day of the week, He first appeared to Mary Magdalene, from whom He had cast out seven demons.

John 20:18: Mary Magdalene came, announcing to the disciples, "I have seen the Lord," and that He had said these things to her.

Luke 24: But at daybreak on the first day of the week [the women] took the spices they had prepared and went to the tomb. They found the stone rolled away from the tomb; but when they entered, they did not find the body of the Lord Jesus. While they were puzzling over this, behold, two men in dazzling garments appeared to them. They were terrified and bowed their faces to the ground. They said to them, "Why do you seek the living one among the dead?

He is not here, but he has been raised. Remember what he said to you while he was still in Galilee, that the Son of Man must be handed over to sinners and be crucified, and rise on the third day." And they remembered his words.

Then they returned from the tomb and announced all these things to the eleven and to all the others.

The women were Mary Magdalene, Joanna, and Mary the mother of James; the others who accompanied them also told this to the apostles, but their story seemed like nonsense and they did not believe them.

It is the myth woven into the story of Mary that empowers her to us. To many, she is the captive, possessed, enslaved, caught in the midst of crime and tragedy, but at once redeemed, set free, and loved by God himself. She is hope and triumph. She represents the power of truth and love to change the life of the lowest and most powerless of us. She is you and me in search of God.

The Reaction of Christendom

Reaction to Gnosticism within the newly forming church was swift and bold. Beginning with a swelling defense in the New Testament itself, the writers began to define and defend doctrine. Labels, names, and descriptions of the Christian doctrine would be established later in various councils, but for now there would be decisive actions to fend off new ideas.

Considering the fact that there were two main approaches to Gnosticism in the first and second centuries, the stoic-ascetic approach of self denial and the hedonistic-epicurean approach of self indulgence, we will find two criticisms mounted against Gnosticism in the Bible. First we will examine the pronouncements against the more hedonistic sects.

2 Timothy 3 (King James Version)

1 This know also, that in the last days perilous times shall come.

2 For men shall be lovers of their own selves, covetous, boasters, proud, blasphemers, disobedient to parents, unthankful, unholy,

3 Without natural affection, trucebreakers, false accusers, incontinent, fierce, despisers of those that are good,

4 Traitors, heady, highminded, lovers of pleasures more than lovers of God;

65

5 Having a form of godliness, but denying the power thereof: from such turn away.

6 For of this sort are they which creep into houses, and lead captive silly women laden with sins, led away with divers lusts,

7 Ever learning, and never able to come to the knowledge of the truth.

Keeping in mind the previous information and scripture given regarding the Gnostic sect of the Nicolaitanes, Timothy mounts an attack against Pagans and wayward Christians, including certain Gnostics, who had fallen into debauchery. The last line of the admonition targets what he sees as the Gnostic weakness of, *"Ever learning, and never able to come to the knowledge of the truth."*

One of the most difficult passages to apprehend is found in 1 John chapter 4, where the writer attempts to draw a fine line between what is the error in Gnostic theology and what is the full truth of Christ on earth according to orthodoxy.

1 John (King James Version)
1 John 4

1 Beloved, believe not every spirit, but try the spirits whether they are of God: because many false prophets are gone out into the world.

2 Hereby know ye the Spirit of God: Every spirit that confesseth that

Jesus Christ is come in the flesh is of God:

3 And every spirit that confesseth not that Jesus Christ is come in the flesh is not of God: and this is that spirit of antichrist, whereof ye have heard that it should come; and even now already is it in the world.

4 Ye are of God, little children, and have overcome them: because greater is he that is in you, than he that is in the world.

5They are of the world: therefore speak they of the world, and the world heareth them.

6 We are of God: he that knoweth God heareth us; he that is not of God heareth not us. Hereby know we the spirit of truth, and the spirit of error.

7 Beloved, let us love one another: for love is of God; and every one that loveth is born of God, and knoweth God.

8 He that loveth not knoweth not God; for God is love.

9 In this was manifested the love of God toward us, because that God sent his only begotten Son into the world, that we might live through him.

10 Herein is love, not that we loved God, but that he loved us, and sent his Son to be the propitiation for our sins.

11 Beloved, if God so loved us, we ought also to love one another.

12 No man hath seen God at any time. If we love one another, God dwelleth in us, and his love is perfected in us.

13 Hereby know we that we dwell in him, and he in us, because he hath given us of his Spirit.

14 *And we have seen and do testify that the Father sent the Son to be the Saviour of the world.*

15 *Whosoever shall confess that Jesus is the Son of God, God dwelleth in him, and he in God.*

16 *And we have known and believed the love that God hath to us. God is love; and he that dwelleth in love dwelleth in God, and God in him.*

17 *Herein is our love made perfect, that we may have boldness in the day of judgment: because as he is, so are we in this world.*

With gentle and elegant words, John cuts to the bone, amputating the part of Christendom seen as heretical.

1 *Beloved, believe not every spirit, but try the spirits whether they are of God: because many false prophets are gone out into the world.*

2 *Hereby know ye the Spirit of God: Every spirit that confesseth that Jesus Christ is come in the flesh is of God:*

3 *And every spirit that confesseth not that Jesus Christ is come in the flesh is not of God: and this is that spirit of antichrist, whereof ye have heard that it should come; and even now already is it in the world.*

The statement above is a direct attack against the Gnostic beliefs regarding Jesus and the Christ spirit. The Gnostic belief that spirit and matter could not co-exist makes it impossible for Christ to inhabit a fleshly body. The belief by some was that Jesus was an illusion or specially prepared body and Christ was somehow separate from Jesus. This made it impossible for the man Jesus to be the literal son of God.

John drives home the differences and calls the differences heresies, proclaiming that those who do not hold to orthodox beliefs have the spirit of the antichrist.

After the establishment of cannon, many incorrectly cited the following chapter to condemn Gnosticism and other religions that seemed to be gaining a notable following. Ironically, Protestants would later use the same verses to condemn Catholicism.

Revelation 17 (King James Version)
1 And there came one of the seven angels which had the seven vials, and talked with me, saying unto me, Come hither; I will shew unto thee the judgment of the great whore that sitteth upon many waters:
2 With whom the kings of the earth have committed fornication, and the inhabitants of the earth have been made drunk with the wine of her fornication.
3 So he carried me away in the spirit into the wilderness: and I saw a woman sit upon a scarlet coloured beast, full of names of blasphemy, having seven heads and ten horns.

4 *And the woman was arrayed in purple and scarlet colour, and decked with gold and precious stones and pearls, having a golden cup in her hand full of abominations and filthiness of her fornication:*

5 *And upon her forehead was a name written, MYSTERY, BABYLON THE GREAT, THE MOTHER OF HARLOTS AND ABOMINATIONS OF THE EARTH.*

6 *And I saw the woman drunken with the blood of the saints, and with the blood of the martyrs of Jesus: and when I saw her, I wondered with great admiration.*

7 *And the angel said unto me, Wherefore didst thou marvel? I will tell thee the mystery of the woman, and of the beast that carrieth her, which hath the seven heads and ten horns.*

8 *The beast that thou sawest was, and is not; and shall ascend out of the bottomless pit, and go into perdition: and they that dwell on the earth shall wonder, whose names were not written in the book of life from the foundation of the world, when they behold the beast that was, and is not, and yet is.*

9 *And here is the mind which hath wisdom. The seven heads are seven mountains, on which the woman sitteth.*

10 *And there are seven kings: five are fallen, and one is, and the other is not yet come; and when he cometh, he must continue a short space.*

11 *And the beast that was, and is not, even he is the eighth, and is of the seven, and goeth into perdition.*

12 And the ten horns which thou sawest are ten kings, which have received no kingdom as yet; but receive power as kings one hour with the beast.

13 These have one mind, and shall give their power and strength unto the beast.

14 These shall make war with the Lamb, and the Lamb shall overcome them: for he is Lord of lords, and King of kings: and they that are with him are called, and chosen, and faithful.

15 And he saith unto me, The waters which thou sawest, where the whore sitteth, are peoples, and multitudes, and nations, and tongues.

16 And the ten horns which thou sawest upon the beast, these shall hate the whore, and shall make her desolate and naked, and shall eat her flesh, and burn her with fire.

17 For God hath put in their hearts to fulfil his will, and to agree, and give their kingdom unto the beast, until the words of God shall be fulfilled.

18 And the woman which thou sawest is that great city, which reigneth over the kings of the earth.

Is the whore of Babylon Mary, as conservative Christians claim? If it is Mary, is it the representation of Mother Mary or that of Mary Magdalene? Is Gnosticism the great heresy that will bring about the downfall of the Christian church?

Let us begin with the writer's concluding statement.

Revelation 17

15 And he saith unto me, The waters which thou sawest, where the whore sitteth, are peoples, and multitudes, and nations, and tongues.

16 And the ten horns which thou sawest upon the beast, these shall hate the whore, and shall make her desolate and naked, and shall eat her flesh, and burn her with fire.

17 For God hath put in their hearts to fulfil his will, and to agree, and give their kingdom unto the beast, until the words of God shall be fulfilled.

18 And the woman which thou sawest is that great city, which reigneth over the kings of the earth.

"The woman you saw is that great city which reigns over the kings of the earth." (Rev 17:18) The great whore is not a person at all, but a place – a city, which is a seat of power wherein kings and nations are ruled.

It is not the purpose of this work to defend Gnosticism, but only to explain it. Within that explanation must be the church's defense against it. After all, until the discovery of the Gnostic gospels we knew nothing of the Gnostics but what the church fathers said about the sect as they defended the church against what they considered to be a great heresy. For those who do not take time to thoroughly research information regarding the sect, they will be confronted with the same biased and limited information as was offered to the masses of the second century.

What we can say about Gnosticism is that it does not fit the pattern to be considered the "great whore" of Revelation, as some have said.

Are Gnostics Christian? Or, to ask the question in another way, is Gnosticism a sect or denomination of Christianity? The answer depends on what prerequisites must be fulfilled in one's faith and doctrine to be considered "Christian."

If the mention or presence of a scared feminine force precludes acceptance, then all of Catholicism would be excluded. Holy Mary, Mother of God now sits sinless on the right hand of Christ as an ascended co-redeemer with him. Having been impregnated by the Holy Spirit, she carried God in her womb and gave birth to God on earth. She lived as a virgin, gave birth, yet remained a virgin, and died as a virgin. She ascended to heaven and took her place, first as an intercessor between man and Christ, then was promoted by the church to the place of co-redeemer with Christ. She is the sacred feminine within the Catholic church.

Must one believe in original sin to be a Christian? The Eastern Orthodox Church does not hold to this doctrine. They believe we have a predisposition to sin, but they do not believe we are born into sin. Are those who follow one of the oldest Christian churches in the world Christians?

Must one believe in the doctrine of the trinity to be a Christian? The Church of Jesus Christ Latter-day Saints and Jehovah's Witnesses do not believe God and Christ are one and the same.

Although these denominations did not exist at the time the Council of Nicea met at Constantine's behest, when Constantine legalized Christianity, the same problem existed. What constitutes Christianity? To answer this question church leaders came together and by majority consent, the Nicene Creed was developed. The creed, written below, became the measuring rod which decided admittance into Christendom. But before and after the great council there have been creeds, and they all have been different.

What is a Christian? To what list of beliefs must one pledge allegiance? It seems the target continued to move over time. What can be said without fail is that those who wrote a creed sought to include their followers and endeavored not to reach too far beyond their basic theology.

Doctrine is constructed for two reasons, to correct error and to form alliances. There were some who believed Jesus was born a man and some who believed he was born a god, and some who didn't believe he was born at all. When constructing the doctrine of the Holy Trinity, the doctrines of Jesus as God and Jesus as man were united. The group who believed he was a spirit and was not born were cast aside. An alliance was formed, and when alliances are formed by some they are usually formed to the exclusion of others.

As points of doctrine are linked together, creeds are formed. These become the bedrock beliefs of the group. Those who do not believe in all points of the creed are considered enemies or outcasts of the group.

Excluded from the new alliance was Arius and his group. Arius taught that Jesus, being the son of God was created by God and was therefore subordinate to him. Arius was a popular figure who had begun to amass a sizable following. Paraphrasing Epiphanius, Arius is described as "tall and lean, of distinguished appearance, and polished address. Women doted on him, charmed by his beautiful manners, touched by his appearance of asceticism. Men were impressed by his aura of intellectual superiority."

When the Council of Nicaea (A.D. 325) rejected the teaching of Arius, it expressed its position by adopting one of the current Eastern symbols and inserting into it some anti-Arian phrases, resulting in this creed. At the Council of Constantinople (A.D. 381) some minor changes were made, and it was reaffirmed at the Council of Chalcedon (A.D. 451). It is an essential part of the doctrine and liturgy of the Lutheran churches. Historically it has been used especially at Holy Communion on Sundays and major feasts (except when the Apostles' Creed is used as the Baptismal Creed).

Let us see how the church constructed creeds in order to articulate its position and exclude some from its numbers.

The Nicene Creed

We believe in one God,
the Father, the Almighty,
maker of heaven and earth,
of all that is, seen and unseen.
We believe in one Lord, Jesus Christ,
the only Son of God,
eternally begotten of the Father,
God from God, Light from Light,
true God from true God,
begotten, not made,
of one Being with the Father.
Through Him all things were made.
For us and for our salvation

He came down from heaven;

by the power of the Holy Spirit

He became incarnate from the Virgin Mary, and was made man.

For our sake He was crucified under Pontius Pilate;

He suffered death and was buried.

On the third day He rose again

in accordance with the Scriptures;

He ascended into heaven

and is seated at the right hand of the Father.

He will come again in glory to judge the living and the dead,

and His kingdom will have no end.

We believe in the Holy Spirit, the Lord, the giver of life,

who proceeds from the Father and the Son.

With the Father and the Son He is worshiped and glorified.

He has spoken through the Prophets.

We believe in one holy catholic and apostolic Church.

We acknowledge one baptism for the forgiveness of sins.

We look for the resurrection of the dead,

and the life of the world to come. Amen.

The Old Roman Creed

AS QUOTED BY TERTULLIAN (c. 200)

De Virginibus Velandis	Tertullian	De Praescriptione
Believing in one God Almighty, maker of the world,	We believe one only God,	I believe in one God, maker of the world,
And His Son, Jesus Christ,	and the son of God Jesus Christ,	the Word, called His Son, Jesus Christ,
Born of the Virgin Mary,	born of the Virgin,	by the Spirit and power of God the Father made flesh in Mary's womb, and born of her
crucified under Pontius Pilate,	Him suffered died, and buried,	fastened to a cross.
on the third day brought to life from the dead,	Brought back to life,	He rose the third day,

received in heaven,	taken again into heaven,	was caught up into heaven,
sitting now at the right hand of the Father,	sits at the right hand of the Father,	set at the right hand of the Father,
will come to judge the living and the dead	will come to judge the living and the dead	will come with glory to take the good into life eternal, and condemn the wicked to perpetual fire,
	who has sent from the Father the Holy Ghost.	sent the vicarious power of His Holy Spirit,
		to govern believers (In this passage articles 9 and 10 precede 8)
through resurrection of the flesh.		restoration of the flesh.

This table serves to show how incomplete the evidence provided is by mere quotations of the Creed, and how cautiously it must be dealt with. Had we possessed only the "De Virginibus Velandis", we might have said that the article concerning the Holy Ghost did not form part of Tertullian's Creed. Had the "De Virginibus Velandis" been destroyed, we should have declared that Tertullian knew nothing of the clause "suffered under Pontius Pilate". And so forth.

While no explicit statement of this composition by the Apostles is forthcoming before the close of the fourth century, earlier fathers such as Tertullian and St. Irenaeus insist that the "rule of faith" is part of the apostolic tradition. Tertullian in particular in his "De Praescriptione" insists that the rule was instituted by Christ and delivered to us by the apostles.

II. The Old Roman Creed

The Catechism of the Council of Trent apparently assumed the apostolic origin of our existing creed. Pointing to the old Roman form as a template, however, if the old Roman form had been held to be the inspired utterance of the Apostles, it would not have been modified too easily at pleasure of the local churches. In particular, it would never have been entirely supplanted by today's form. Printing them side-by-side best reveals the difference between the two:

Roman	Today
(1) I believe in God the Father Almighty;	(1) I believe in God the Father Almighty *Creator of Heaven and earth*
(2) And in Jesus Christ, His only Son, our Lord;	(2) And in Jesus Christ, His only Son, our Lord;

(3) Who was born of (de) the Holy Ghost and of (ex) the Virgin Mary;	(3) Who was *conceived* by the Holy Ghost, born of the Virgin Mary,
(4) Crucified under Pontius Pilate and buried;	(4) *Suffered* under Pontius Pilate, was crucified, *dead*, and buried;
(5) The third day He rose again from the dead,	(5) *He descended into hell*; the third day He rose again from the dead;
(6) He ascended into Heaven,	(6) He ascended into Heaven, sitteth at the right hand of <u>God</u> the Father *Almighty*;
(7) Sitteth at the right hand of the Father,	(7) From thence He shall come to judge the living and the dead.
(8) Whence He shall come to judge the living and the dead.	(8) *I believe* in the Holy Ghost,

(9) And in the Holy Ghost,	(9) The Holy *Catholic* Church, *the communion of saints*
(10) The Holy Church,	(10) The forgiveness of sins,
(11) The forgiveness of sins;	(11) The resurrection of the body, and
(12) The resurrection of the body.	(12) *life everlasting.*

Please note that the Roman form does not contain the clauses "Creator of heaven and earth", "descended into hell", "the communion of saints", "life everlasting", nor the words "conceived", "suffered", "died", and "Catholic." Many of these additions were probably known to St. Jerome in Palestine (c. 380.--See Morin in Revue Benedictine, January, 1904) Further additions appear in the creeds of southern Gaul at the beginning of the next century, but Tertullian probably assumed its final shape in Rome itself some time before A.D. 700 (Burn, Introduction, 239; and Journal of Theology Studies, July, 1902). We are not certain as to the reasons leading to the changes, but it could be speculated that they were written as implicit

83

defenses of heresies that were popular throughout the time of the alterations.

The Apostles' Creed

The Apostles' Creed, as we have it now, dates from the eighth century. However, it is a revision of the so-called Old Roman Creed, which was used in the West by the third century. Behind the Old Roman Creed, in turn, were variations, which had roots in the New Testament itself. While this creed does not come from the apostles, its roots are apostolic. It serves as a Baptismal symbol in that it describes the faith into which we are baptized and is used in the rites of Baptism and Affirmation of Baptism.

I believe in God, the Father almighty,
creator of heaven and earth.
I believe in Jesus Christ, His only Son, our Lord.
He was conceived by the power of the Holy Spirit
and born of the Virgin Mary.
He suffered under Pontius Pilate,
was crucified, died, and was buried.
He descended into hell.*

On the third day he rose again.

He ascended into heaven,

and is seated at the right hand of the Father.

He will come again to judge the living and the dead.

I believe in the Holy Spirit,

the holy catholic Church,

the communion of saints,

the forgiveness of sins,

the resurrection of the body,

and the life everlasting. Amen.

*or "He descended to the dead."

Text prepared by the International Consultation on English Texts (ICET) and the English Language Liturgical Consultation (ELLC). Reproduced by permission.

This exposition of the creed was made at the request of Laurentius, a Bishop whose see is unknown, but is conjectured by Fontanini, in his life of Rufinus, to have been Concordia, Rufinus' birthplace. Here is the English translation of the creed, which Rufinus was asked to make commentary on. The date of the writing was about 307 A.D.

I believe in God the Father Almighty, invisible and impassible. And in Jesus Christ, His only Son, our Lord; Who was born from the Holy

Ghost, of the Virgin Mary; Was crucified under Pontius Pilate, and buried; He descended to hell; on the third day He rose again from the dead. He ascended to the heavens; He sitteth at the right hand of the Father; Thence He is to come to judge the quick and the dead. And in the Holy Ghost; The Holy Church. The remission of sins. The resurrection of this flesh.

The Chalcedonian Creed

The Chalcedonian Creed was adopted in the fifth century, at the Council of Chalcedon in 451, which is one of the seven Ecumenical councils accepted by Eastern Orthodox, Catholic, and many Protestant Christian churches.

We, then, following the holy Fathers, all with one consent, teach men to confess one and the same Son, our Lord Jesus Christ, the same perfect in Godhead and also perfect in manhood; truly God and truly man, of a reasonable [rational] soul and body; consubstantial [co-essential] with the Father according to the Godhead, and consubstantial with us according to the Manhood; in all things like unto us, without sin; begotten before all ages of the Father according to the Godhead, and in these latter days, for us and for our salvation, born of the Virgin Mary, the Mother of God, according to the Manhood; one and the same Christ, Son, Lord, only begotten, to be acknowledged in two natures, unconfusedly, unchangeably, indivisibly, inseparably; the distinction of natures being by no means taken away by the union, but rather the property of each nature being preserved, and concurring in one Person and one Subsistence, not parted or divided into two persons, but one and the same Son, and only begotten, God the Word, the Lord Jesus Christ; as the prophets from the beginning [have declared] concerning Him, and the Lord Jesus Christ Himself has taught us, and the Creed of the holy Fathers has handed down to us.

The Athanasian Creed

This creed is of uncertain origin. It was supposedly prepared in the time of Athanasius, the great theologian of the fourth century, although it seems more likely that it dates from the fifth or sixth centuries and is Western in character. It assists the Church in combating two errors that undermined Bible teaching: the denial that God's Son and the Holy Spirit are of one being with the Father; the other a denial that Jesus Christ is true God and true man in one person. It declares that whoever rejects the doctrine of the Trinity and the doctrine of Christ is without the saving faith. Traditionally it is considered the "Trinitarian Creed" and read aloud in corporate worship on Trinity Sunday.

Whoever wants to be saved should above all cling to the catholic faith.

Whoever does not guard it whole and inviolable will doubtless perish eternally.

Now this is the catholic faith: We worship one God in Trinity and the Trinity in unity, neither confusing the persons nor dividing the divine being.

For the Father is one person, the Son is another, and the Spirit is still another.

But the deity of the Father, Son, and Holy Spirit is one, equal in glory, coeternal in majesty.

What the Father is, the Son is, and so is the Holy Spirit.

Uncreated is the Father; uncreated is the Son; uncreated is the Spirit.

The Father is infinite; the Son is infinite; the Holy Spirit is infinite.

Eternal is the Father; eternal is the Son; eternal is the Spirit:

And yet there are not three eternal beings, but one who is eternal;

as there are not three uncreated and unlimited beings, but one who is uncreated and unlimited.

Almighty is the Father; almighty is the Son; almighty is the Spirit:

And yet there are not three almighty beings, but one who is almighty.

Thus the Father is God; the Son is God; the Holy Spirit is God:

And yet there are not three gods, but one God.

Thus the Father is Lord; the Son is Lord; the Holy Spirit is Lord:

And yet there are not three lords, but one Lord.

As Christian truth compels us to acknowledge each distinct person as God and Lord, so catholic religion forbids us to say that there are three gods or lords.

The Father was neither made nor created nor begotten;

the Son was neither made nor created, but was alone begotten of the Father;

the Spirit was neither made nor created, but is proceeding from the Father and the Son.

Thus there is one Father, not three fathers; one Son, not three sons; one Holy Spirit, not three spirits.

And in this Trinity, no one is before or after, greater or less than the other;

but all three persons are in themselves, coeternal and coequal; and so we must worship the Trinity in unity and the one God in three persons.

Whoever wants to be saved should think thus about the Trinity.

It is necessary for eternal salvation that one also faithfully believes that our Lord Jesus Christ became flesh.

For this is the true faith that we believe and confess: That our Lord Jesus Christ, God's Son, is both God and man.

He is God, begotten before all worlds from the being of the Father, and He is man, born in the world from the being of his mother -- existing fully as God, and fully as man with a rational soul and a human body; equal to the Father in divinity, subordinate to the Father in humanity.

Although He is God and man, He is not divided, but is one Christ. He is united because God has taken humanity into himself; He does not transform deity into humanity. He is completely one in the unity of his person, without confusing his natures. For as the rational soul and body are one person, so the one Christ is God and man.

He suffered death for our salvation.
He descended into hell and rose again from the dead.
He ascended into heaven and is seated at the right hand of the Father.
He will come again to judge the living and the dead.
At his coming all people shall rise bodily to give an account of their own deeds.
Those who have done good will enter eternal life,
those who have done evil will enter eternal fire.
This is the catholic faith.

One cannot be saved without believing this firmly and faithfully.

Text prepared by the International Consultation on English Texts (ICET) and the English Language Liturgical Consultation (ELLC). Reproduced by permission.

As seen in the examination of these creeds or statements of faith, there is a tendency to expand and change creeds to defend against and virtually close the doors to heresies that rear their heads throughout the existence of the creeds. Thus, just as doctrines spring into existence as an argument and defense against errors in the faith, so creeds change for the same purpose. This sprawl tends to be destructive for several reasons, not the least of which is expanding creeds take expanded time to understand and defend each area of belief. Man's ability to corrupt is endless and man's heresies are endless, thus, in time a creed could expand to become longer than the scripture itself. Expanding creeds takes away from the other areas such as worship and prayer in our spiritual lives.

The simple answer is to understand that if the Holy Spirit were guiding all of us, we would be in one accord as a team under the same harness and reins. To worry about others and our defense against their errors is to weaken our own faith by spending less time with Him who guides us away from error. We cannot stop others from proceeding into error. We can only assure we will not go into error by fully understanding the few fast and hard beliefs held firm by those who came before; and using them as guidelines to ensure ourselves a clear view and understanding of the Christian faith.

When it comes to doctrine, to those that believe, no explanation is necessary, but for those who do not believe, no explanation will suffice.

To the Gnostics, their doctrine and creed were a search for truth within themselves. It was their view of the impregnable line of delineation between matter and spirit that caused issue with the established church. The Supreme God cannot be soiled in any way by the material world. Christ could not be man. God could not be known by corporeal beings. The Holy Spirit could not have impregnated Mary. Christ could not have died because spirits do not die. The resurrection was an illusion.

As the orthodox church designed creeds to define themselves, they served as bricks within a wall that separated Gnosticism from the church forever.

History of the Gospel of Philip

The Gospel of Philip is assumed to be one of the sources of Dan Brown's novel, *The Da Vinci Code*, about Mary Magdalene, Jesus, and their children. The Gospel is one of the Gnostic texts found at Nag Hammadi in Egypt in 1945 and belongs to the same collection of Gnostic documents as the more famous Gospel of Thomas.

It has been suggested that the *Gospel of Philip* was written in the second century A.D. If so, it may be one of the earliest documents containing themes that would later be used in apocryphal literature. This is literature that describes the end of the world or the coming of the heavenly kingdom.

A single manuscript of the *Gospel of Philip*, written in Coptic, was found in the Nag Hammadi library. The collection was a library of thirteen papyrus texts discovered near the town of Nag Hammadi in 1945 by a peasant boy. The writings in these codices comprised 52 documents, most of which are Gnostic in nature.

The codices were probably hidden by monks from the nearby monastery of St. Pachomius when the official Christian Church banned all Gnostic literature around the year 390 A.D

It is believed the original texts were written in Greek during the first or second centuries A.D. The copies contained in the discovered clay jar were written in Coptic in the third or fourth centuries A.D.

From the time Gnosticism was labeled a heresy, the church began a policy of conversion or extermination. Beginning around 390 A.D. and continuing until the Cathar extermination, the church opposed Gnosticism and all movements, forms, and sects that proceeded from it.

In 1209 Pope Innocent III proclaimed a crusade against the last vestiges of "Gnostic-like" sects, the Cathars. For years the church discussed the Cathars, attempting to decide if they could be considered Christian or not. Eventually they would be labeled heretical and ordered to come into line with the orthodox beliefs of the Catholic Church. The Cathars held to their beliefs. Their doctrine included the belief that the world was split along lines of matter and spirit, good and evil. As with many Gnostic sects, they believed in abstaining from the world by purifying themselves, living a life of chastity and poverty. They believed in the equality of the sexes. The Pope saw the Cathars as a danger to the church since the members were admired for their modest lifestyle and the Cathar membership was growing.

Even though the Cathars were an ascetic sect, leading lives of peace and abstinence, they were hunted down and killed. Twenty years of carnage and warfare followed in which cities and provinces throughout the south of France were systematically eradicated. In an attempt to kill every Cathar, one of the worst episodes of the war ensued when the entire population of Toulouse, both Cathar and Catholic, were massacred. In 1243 the Cathar fortress of Montsegur in the Pyrenees was captured and destroyed. Those who refused to renounce their beliefs were tortured or put to death by fire. In spite of continued persecution, the Cathar movement continued through the 14th century, finally disappearing in the 15th century. Still, the church could not find or destroy all Gnostic literature. Books such as *The Gospel of Philip* remained.

The *Gospel Of Philip* is a list of sayings focusing on man's redemption and salvation as framed by Gnostic theology, and is presented here based on a comparative study of translations from the Nag Hammadi Codex by Wesley W. Isenberg, Willis Barnstone, The Ecumenical Coptic Project, Bart Ehrman, Marvin Meyer, David Cartlidge, David Dungan, and other sources.

Each verse was weighed against the theological and philosophical beliefs held by the Gnostic community at the time in which the document was penned. All attempts were made to render the most accurate meaning based on the available translations and information.

Exact wording was secondary to the conveyance of the overall meaning as understood by the contemporary reader.

When the wording of a verse held two possible meanings or needed expanded definitions, optional translations were placed in parentheses.

The Gospel of Philip

1. A Hebrew makes a Hebrew convert, and they call him a proselyte (novice). A novice does not make another novice.

Some are just as they are, and they make others like themselves to receive. It is enough for them that they simply are as they are.

2. The slave seeks only to be set free. He does not hope to attain the estate of his master. The son acts as a son (heir), but the father gives the inheritance to him.

3. Those who inherit the dead are dead, and they inherit the dead. Those who inherit the living are alive. They inherit both the living and the dead.

The dead cannot inherit anything. How can the dead inherit anything? When the dead inherits the living one, he shall not die but the dead shall live instead.

4. The Gentile (unbeliever) who does not believe does not die, because he has never been alive, so he could not die. He who has trusted the Truth has found life and is in danger of dying, because he is now alive.

5. Since the day that the Christ came, the cosmos was created, the cities are built (adorned), and the dead carried out (disposed of).

6. In the days when we were Hebrews we were made orphans, having only our Mother. Yet when we believed in the Messiah (and became the ones of Christ), the Mother and Father both came to us.

7. Those who sow in the winter reap in the summer. The winter is this world system. The summer is the other age or dispensation (to come). Let us sow in the world (cosmos) so that we will reap in the summer. Because of this, it is right for us not to pray in the winter. What comes from (follows) the winter is the summer. If anyone reaps in the winter he will not harvest but rather pull it up by the roots and will not produce fruit. Not only does it not produce in winter, but on the Sabbath his field shall be bare.

8. The Christ has come to fully ransom some, to save (restore and heal) others, and to be the propitiation (payment) for others. Those who were estranged he ransomed. He purchases them for himself. He saves, heals, and restores those who come to him. These he desires to pledge (in marriage). When he became manifest (in this world) he ordained the soul (with a body) as he desired (and set aside his own life), but even before this, in the time of the world's beginning, he had ordained the soul (he had laid down his own life for these souls). At his appointed time he came to bring the soul he pledged himself to back to (for) himself. It had come to be under the control of robbers and they took it captive. Yet he saved it, and he paid the price for both the good and the evil of the world.

9. Light and dark, life and death, right and left are brothers. It is impossible for one to be separated from the other. They are neither good, nor evil. A life is not alive without death. Death is not death if one were not alive. Therefore each individual shall be returned to his origin, as he was from the beginning. Those who go beyond the world will live forever and are in the eternal present.

10. The names that are given to worldly things cause great confusion. They contort our perception from the real to the unreal. He who hears the word "God" does not think of the real, but rather has false, preconceived ideas. It is the same with the words "Father," "Son," "Holy Spirit," "Life," "Light," "Resurrection," and "Church (the called out ones)," and all other words. They do not recall the real, but rather they call to mind preconceived, false ideas.

They (Archons) learned the reality of human death. They (Archons) who are in the world system made them (men) think of the false idea. If they had been in eternity, they would not have designated anything as evil, nor would they have placed things within worldly events (time and place). They (men) are destined for eternity.

11. The only name they (men) should never speak into the world is the name the Father gave himself through the Son. This is the Father's name. It exists that he may be exalted over all things. The Son could not become the Father, unless he was given the Father's name. This name exists so that they (men) may have it in their thoughts. They (men) should never speak it. Those who do not have it cannot even think it. But

the truth created names in the world for our sake. It would not be possible to learn the truth without names.

12. The Truth alone is the truth. It is a single thing and a multitude of things. The truth teaches us love alone through many and varied paths.

13. Those who ruled (lower gods) desired to deceive man because they knew man was related to the truly good ones. They (Archons) took the designation of good and they gave it to those who were not good. They did this so that by way of words they might deceive man and bind him to those who are not good. When they receive favor, they are taken from those who are not good and placed among the good. These are they who had recognized themselves. The rulers (lower gods) had desired to take the free person, and enslave him to themselves forever. Rulers of power fight against man. The rulers do not want him to be saved (recognize himself), so that men will become their masters. For if man is saved there will be no need for sacrifice.

14. When sacrifice began, animals were offered up to the ruling powers (Archon / Demiurge). They were offered up to them while the sacrificial animals were still alive. But as

they offered them up they were killed. But the Christ was offered up dead to God (the Supreme God), and yet he lived.

15. Before the Christ came, there had been no bread in the world. In paradise, the place where Adam was, there had been many plants as food for wild animals, but paradise had no wheat for man to eat. Man had to be nourished like animals. But the Christ, the perfect man, was sent. He brought the bread of heaven, so that man could eat as he should.

16. The rulers (lower gods) thought what they did (create the material world) was by their own will and power, but the Holy Spirit worked through them without their knowledge to do her will.

17. The truth, which exists from the beginning, is sown everywhere, and everyone sees it being sown, but only a few see the harvest.

18. Some say that Mary conceived (impregnated) by the Holy Spirit. They are in error. They do not know what they are saying. How can a female impregnate another female? (The Holy Spirit is a feminine force.) Mary is the virgin whom no

power defiled. She is a great problem and curse among the Hebrew Apostles and those in charge (church leaders). The ruler (lower god) who attempts to defile this virgin, is himself defiled. The Lord was not going to say, "my father in heaven", unless he really had another father (on earth). He would simply have said, "my father".

19. The Lord says to the Disciples, "Come into the house of the Father, but do not bring anything in or take anything out from the father's house."

20. Jesus (Yeshua) is the secret name; Christ (messiah) is the revealed name. The name "Jesus" (Yeshua) does not occur in any other language. His name is called "Jesus" (Yeshua). In Aramaic his name is Messiah, but in Greek it is Christ (Cristos). In every language he is called the anointed one. The fact that he is Savior (Yeshua) could be fully comprehended only by himself, since it is the Nazarene who reveals the secret things.

21. Christ has within himself all things; man, angel, mystery (sacraments), and the father.

22. Those who say that the Lord first died and then arose are in error. He would have to first arise (be born) before he could die. If he is not first resurrected (born) he would die, but God lives and cannot die.

(Alternate translation:
Those who say that the Lord died first and then arose are in error. He arose first and then died. If one does not first attain the resurrection, he will not die. As God lives, he would live also).

23. No one will hide something highly valuable in something ostentatious (that would draw attention). More often, one places something of great worth within a number of containers worth nothing. This is how it is with the (human) soul. It is a precious thing placed within a lowly body.

24. Some are fearful that they will arise (from the dead) naked. Therefore they desire to rise in the flesh. They do not understand that those who choose to wear the flesh are naked (destitute in spirit). Those who choose to strip themselves of the flesh are the ones who are not naked.

25. Flesh and blood will not be able to inherit the kingdom of God. What is this that will not inherit? It is that which is upon each of us (our flesh). But what will inherit the kingdom is that which belongs to Jesus and is of his flesh and blood. Therefore he says: "He who does not eat my flesh and drink my blood, has no life in him." What is his flesh? It is the Word, and his blood is the Holy Spirit. He who has received these has food and drink and clothing.

26. I disagree with those who say the flesh will not arise. They are in error. Tell me what will rise so that we may honor you. You say it is the spirit in the flesh and the light contained in the flesh. But whatever you say there is nothing you mention that is contained outside of the flesh (material world). It is necessary to arise in this flesh if everything exists within the flesh (and everything exists as part of or connected to the material world).

27. In this world those wearing a garment are more valuable than the garment. In the kingdom of the Heavens the garment is more valuable than the one wearing it.

28. By water and fire the entire realm is purified through the revelations by those who reveal them, and by the secrets

through those who keep them. Yet, there are things kept secret even within those things revealed. There is water in baptism and there is fire in the oil of anointing.

29. Jesus took them all by surprise. For he did not reveal himself as he originally was, but he revealed himself as they were capable of perceiving him. He revealed himself to all in their own way. To the great, he revealed himself as great. To the small he was small. He revealed himself to the angels as an angel and to mankind he was a man. Some looked at him and saw themselves. But, throughout all of this, he concealed his words from everyone. However when he revealed himself to his Disciples upon the mountain, he appeared glorious. He was not made small. He became great, but he also made the disciples great so that they would be capable of comprehending his greatness.

30. He said on that day during his thanksgiving (in the Eucharist), "You have combined the perfect light and the holy spirit along with angels and images."

31. Do not hate the Lamb. Without him it is not possible to see the door to the sheepfold. Those who are naked will not come before the King.

32. The Sons of the Heavenly Man are more numerous than those of the earthly man. If the sons of Adam are numerous although they die, think of how many more Sons the Perfect Man has and these do not die. And they are continually born every instant of time.

33. The Father creates a son, but it is not possible for the son to create a son because it is impossible for someone who was just born to have a child. The Son has brothers, not sons.

34. There is order in things. All those who are born in the world are begotten physically. Some are begotten spiritually, fed by the promise of heaven, which is delivered by the perfect Word from the mouth. The perfect Word is conceived through a kiss and thus they are born. There is unction to kiss one another to receive conception from grace to grace.

35. There were three women named Mary (Bitter) who walked with the Lord all the time. They were his mother, his sister and Mary of Magdala, who was his consort (companion). Thus his mother, his sister and companion (consort) were all named Mary.

36. "Father" and "Son" are single names, "Holy Spirit" is a double name and it is everywhere; above and below, secret and revealed. The Holy Spirit's abode is manifest when she is below. When she is above she is hidden.

(Alternative translation:
"Father" and "Son" are single names; "Holy Spirit" is a double name. For they are everywhere: they are above, they are below; they are concealed, they are revealed. When the Holy Spirit is in the revealed it is below. When it is in the concealed it is above.)

37. Saints are served by evil powers (lesser gods). The evil spirits are deceived by the Holy Spirit. They think they are assisting a common man when they are serving Saints. A follower of the Lord once asked him for a thing from this world. He answered him saying, "Ask your Mother, and she will give you something from another realm."

38. The Apostles said to the students, "May all of our offering obtain salt!" They had called Sophia (wisdom) salt and without it no offering can become acceptable.

39. Sophia (wisdom) is barren. She has no children but she is called Mother. Others are found (adopted) by the Holy Spirit, and she has many children.

40. That which the Father has belongs to the Son, but he cannot possess it when he is young (small). When he comes of age all his father has will be given to the son.

41. Those who do not follow the path are born of the Spirit, and they stray because of her. By this same spirit (breath or life force), the fire blazes and consumes.

42. Earthly wisdom is one thing, and earthly wisdom (death) is another. Earthly wisdom is simply wisdom, but death is the wisdom of death, and death is the one who understands death. Being familiar with death is minor wisdom.

43. There are animals like the bull and donkey that are submissive to man. There are others that live in the wilderness. Man plows the field with submissive animals, and uses the harvest to feed himself as well as all the animals, domesticated or wild. So it is with the Perfect Man. Through submissive powers he plows and provides for all

things to exist. He causes all things to come together into existence, whether good or evil, right or left.

44. The Holy Spirit is the shepherd guiding everyone and every power (lower ruler or lesser gods), whether submissive, rebellious, or feral. She controls them, subdues them, and keeps them bridled, whether they wish it or not.

45. He who was created (Adam) is beautiful. One would not expect his children to be noble. If he were not created but rather born, one would expect his children to be noble. But he was both created and born. Is this nobility?

46. Adultery occurred first and then came murder. And Cain was conceived in adultery because he was the serpent's (Satan's) son. He became a murderer just like his father. He killed his brother. When copulation occurs between those who are not alike, this is adultery.

47. God is a dyer. Just as a good and true dye penetrates deep into fabric to dye it permanently from within (not a surface act), so God has baptized what He dyes into an indelible dye, which is water.

48. It is impossible for anyone to see anything in the real world, unless he has become part of it. It is not like a person in this world. When one looks at the sun he can see it without being part of it. He can see the sky or the earth or anything without having to be part of it. So it is with this world, but in the other world you must become what you see (see what you become). To see spirit you must be spirit. To see Christ you must be Christ. To see the Father you must be the Father. In this way you will see everything but yourself. If you look at yourself you will become what you see.

49. Faith receives, but love gives. No one can receive without faith. No one can love without giving. Believe and you shall receive. Love and you shall give. If you give without love, you shall receive nothing. Whoever has not received the Lord, continues to be a Hebrew.

50. The Apostles who came before us called him Jesus, The Nazarene, and The Messiah. Of these names, Jesus (Yeshua), The Nazarene (of the rite of the Nazarites), and The Messiah (Christ), the last name is the Christ, the first is Jesus, and the middle name is The Nazarene. Messiah has two meanings; the anointed one and the measured one. Jesus (Yeshua) means The Atonement (redemption or payment). 'Nazara'

means Truth. Therefore, the Nazarite is The Truth. The Christ is The Measured One, the Nazarite (Truth) and Jesus (Redemption) have been measured (are the measurement).

51. The pearl which is thrown into the mud is not worth less than it was before. If it is anointed with balsam oil it is valued no higher. It is as valuable as its owner perceives it to be. So it is with the children of God. Whatever becomes of them, they are precious in their Father's eyes.

52. If you say you are a Jew it will not upset anyone. If you say you are a Roman no one will care. If you claim to be a Greek, foreigner, slave, or a free man no one will be the least bit disturbed. But, if you claim to belong to Christ everyone will take heed (be concerned). I hope to receive this title from him. Those who are worldly would not be able to endure when they hear the name.

53. God is a man-eater (cannibal), because men are sacrificed to him. Before men were sacrificed, animals were sacrificed. Those to whom they are sacrificed are not gods.

54. Vessels of glass and vessels of clay are always made with fire. But if a glass vessel should break it is recast, because it is

made in a single breath. If a clay vessel breaks it is destroyed, since it came into being without breath.

55. A donkey turning a millstone walked a hundred miles but when it was untied it was in the same place it started. There are those who go on long journeys but do not progress. When evening comes (when the journey ends), they have discovered no city, no village, no construction site, no creature (natural thing), no power (ruler), and no angel. They labored and toiled for nothing (emptiness).

56. The thanksgiving (Eucharist) is Jesus. For in Aramaic they call him farisatha, which means, "to be spread out." This is because Jesus came to crucify the world.

57. The Lord went into the place where Levi worked as a dyer. He took 72 pigments and threw them into a vat. When he drew out the result it was pure white. He said, "This is how the Son of Man has come. He is a dyer."

58. Sophia (Wisdom), which they call barren, is the mother of the angels. And the companion (Consort) was Mary of Magdala. The Lord loved Mary more than all the other disciples and he kissed her often on her mouth (the text is

missing here and the word "mouth" is assumed). The others saw his love for Mary and asked him: "Why do you love her more than all of us?" The Savior replied, "Why do I not love you in the same way I love her?" While a blind person and a person who sees are both in the dark, there is no difference, but when the light comes, the one who sees shall behold the light, but he who is blind will remain in darkness.

59. The Lord says: "Blessed is he who existed before you came into being, for he is and was and shall (continue to) be."

60. The supremacy of man is not evident, but it is hidden. Because of this he is master of the animals, which are stronger (larger) than him, in ways both evident and not. This allows the animals to survive. But, when man departs from them, they bite and kill and devour each other because they have no food. Now they have food because man cultivated the land.

61. If one goes down into the water (is baptized) and comes up having received nothing, but claims to belong to Christ, he has borrowed against the name at a high interest rate. But if one receives the Holy Spirit, he has been given the name as a gift. He who has received a gift does not have to pay for it

or give it back. If you have borrowed the name you will have to pay it back with interest when it is demanded. This is how the mystery works.

62. Marriage is a sacrament and a mystery. It is grand. For the world is founded upon man, and man founded upon marriage. Consider sex (pure sex), it has great power although its image is defiled.

63. Among the manifestations of unclean spirits there are male and female. The males are those who mate with the souls inhabiting a female form, and the female spirits invite those inhabiting a male form to have sex. Once seized, no one escapes unless they receive both the male and female power that is endued to the Groom with the Bride. The power is seen in the mirrored Bridal-Chamber. When foolish women see a man sitting alone, they want to subdue him, touch and handle him, and defile him. When foolish men see a beautiful woman sitting alone, they wish to seduce her, draw her in with desire and defile her. But, if the spirits see the man sitting together with his woman, the female spirit cannot intrude upon the man and the male spirit cannot intrude upon the woman. When image and angel are mated, no one can come between the man and woman.

64. He who comes out from the world cannot be stopped. Because he was once in the world he is now beyond both yearning (desire) and fear. He has overcome the flesh and has mastered envy and desire. If he does not leave the world there are forces that will come to seize him, strangle him. How can anyone escape? How can he fear them? Many times men will come and say, "We are faithful, and we hid from unclean and demonic spirits." But if they had been given the Holy Spirit, no unclean spirit would have clung to them. Do not fear the flesh, nor love it. If you fear it, the flesh will become your master. If you love it, the flesh will devour you and render you unable to move.

65. One exists either in this world or in the resurrection or in transition between them. Do not be found in transition. In that world there is both good and evil. The good in it is not good and the evil in it is not evil. There is evil after this world, which is truly evil and it is called the transition. This is what is called death. While we are in this world it is best that we be born into the resurrection, so that we take off the flesh and find rest and not wander within the region of the transition. Many go astray along the way. Because of this, it is best to go forth from the world before one has sinned.

66. Some neither wish nor are able to act. Others have the will to act but it is best for them if they do not act, because the act they desire to perform would make them a sinner. By not desiring to do a righteous act justice is withheld (justice is not obvious). However, the will always comes before the act. (It is not the act but the will that matters.)

67. An Apostle saw in a vision people confined to a blazing house, held fast in bonds of fire, crying out as flames came from their breath. There was water in the house, and they cried out, "The waters can truly save us." They were misled by their desire. This is called the outermost darkness.
(Alternate translation:
An Apostle saw in a vision people confined to a blazing house, held fast in bonds of fire, lying in the flames. There was water, but they had no faith and did not desire to be saved. They received punishment, being cast into outer darkness.)

68. Soul and spirit were born of water and fire. From water, fire, and light the children of the Bridal-Chamber are born. The fire is the spirit (anointing), the light is the fire, but not

the kind of fire that has form. I speak of the other kind whose form is white and it rains down beauty and splendor.

69. The truth did not come into the world naked, but it came in types and symbols. The world would not receive it any other way. There is a rebirth together with its symbols. One cannot be reborn through symbols. What can the symbol of resurrection raise, or the Bridal-Chamber with its symbols? One must come into the truth through the (true) image (not the symbol or type of it). Truth is this Restoration. It is good for those not born to take on the names of the Father, the Son, and the Holy Spirit. They could not have done so on their own. Whoever is not born of them will have the name (Christ's ones) removed from him. The one who receives them receives the anointing of the spirit and the unction and power of the cross. This is what the Apostles call having the right with the left. When this happens, you no longer belong to Christ, you will be Christ.

70. The Lord did everything through sacraments (mysteries or symbols): There was baptism, anointing, thanksgiving (Eucharist), atonement (sacrifice or payment), and Bridal-Chamber.

71. He says: "I came to make what is inside the same as the outside and what is below as it is above. I came to bring all of this into one place." He revealed himself through types and symbols. Those who say Christ comes from the place beyond (above) are confused.

72. He who is manifest in heaven is called "one from below." And He who knows the hidden thing is He who is above him. The correct way to say it would be "the inner and the outer or this which is beyond the outer." Because of this, the Lord called destruction "the outer darkness." There is nothing beyond it. He says, "My Father, who is in secret." He says, "Go into your inner chamber, shut the door behind you and there pray to your Father who is in secret; He who is deep within." He who is within them all is the Fullness. Beyond Him there is nothing deeper within. The deepest place within is called the uppermost place.

73. Before Christ some came forth. They were not able to go back from where they came. They were no longer able to leave from where they went. Then Christ came. Those who went in he brought out, and those who went out he brought in.

74. When Eve was still within Adam (man), there had been no death. When she was separated from him, death began. If she were to enter him again and if he were to receive her completely, death would stop.

75. "My God, my God, Oh Lord why did you abandon me?" He spoke these words on the cross. He departed (divided) the place and was not there any longer.

76. The Lord arose from the dead. He became as he had been, but his body had been made perfect. He was clothed in true flesh. Our flesh is not true, but rather an image of true flesh, as one beholds in a mirror.

77. The Bridal-Chamber is not for beasts, slaves, or whores. It is for free men and virgins.

78. Through the Holy Spirit we are born again, conceived in Christ, anointed in the spirit, united within us. Only with light can we see ourselves reflected in water or mirror. We are baptized in water and light. It is the light that is the oil of the anointing.

79. There had been three offering vestibules in Jerusalem. One opened to the west called the holy, another opened to the south called the holy of the holy, the third opened to the east called the holy of the holies where the high priest alone was to enter. The Baptism is the holy, the redemption (payment or atonement) is the holy of the holy, and the holy of the holies is the Bridal-Chamber. The Baptism has within it the resurrection and the redemption. Redemption allows entrance into the Bridal-Chamber. The Bridal-Chamber is more exalted than any of these. Nothing compares.

80. Those who pray for Jerusalem love Jerusalem. They are in Jerusalem and they see it now. These are called the holy of the holies.

81. Before the curtain of the Temple was torn we could not see the Bridal-Chamber. All we had was the symbol of the place in heaven. When the curtain was torn from the top to the bottom it made a way for some to ascend.

82. Those who have been clothed in the Perfect Light cannot be seen by the powers, nor can the powers subdue them. Yet one shall be clothed with light in the sacrament (mystery) of sex (union / being united).

83. If the woman had not been separated from the man, neither would have died. Christ came to rectify the error of separation that had occurred. He did this by re-uniting them and giving life to those who died. The woman unites with her husband in the Bridal-Chamber and those who have united in the Bridal-Chamber will not be parted again. Eve separated from Adam because she did not unite with him in the Bridal-Chamber.

84. The soul of man (Adam) was created when breath (spirit) was blown into him. The elements were supplied by his mother (Sophia). When soul (mind or will) became spirit and were joined together he spoke words the powers could not understand. They envied him, his spiritual partner, and his opportunity. They wanted it all for themselves but the Bridal-Chamber was hidden from them.

85. Jesus manifested beside the River Jordan with fullness of the kingdom of the Heavens, which existed before anything. Moreover, he was born as a Son before birth. He was anointed and he anointed. He was atoned and he atoned for others.

86. It is right to speak of a mystery. The Father of them all mated with the Virgin who had come down. A fire shone over him on that day. He revealed the power of the Bridal-Chamber. Because of this power his body came into being on that day. He came forth in the Bridal-Chamber in glory because of the essence that issued forth from the Bridegroom to the Bride. This is how Jesus established everything. It was in his heart. In this same way it is right for each one of the disciples to enter into his rest.

87. Adam came into being from two virgins, from the Spirit and from the virgin earth. Christ was born from a virgin, so that the error which occurred in the beginning would be corrected by him.

88. There were two trees in paradise. One produced beasts, the other produced man. Adam ate from the tree that produced beasts becoming a beast he gave birth to beasts. Because of this, animals were worshipped. God created man and men created gods. This is how the world works; men create gods and they worship their creations. It would have been more appropriate for gods to worship mankind. This would be the way if Adam had not eaten from the tree of life, which bore people.

89. The deeds of man follow his abilities. These are his strengths and the things he does with ease. His result is his children who came forth from his times of rest. His work is governed by his work but in his rest he brings forth his sons. This is the sign and symbol, doing works with strength, and producing children in his rest.

90. In this world the slaves are forced to serve the free. In the kingdom of Heaven the free shall serve the slaves and the Bridegroom of the Bridal-Chamber shall serve the guests. Those of the Bridal-Chamber have a single name among them, it is "rest" and they have no need for any other. The contemplation of the symbol brings enlightenment and great glory. Within those in the Chamber (rest) the glories are fulfilled.

91. Go into the water but do not go down into death, because Christ shall atone for him when he who is baptized comes forth. They were called to be fulfilled in his name. For he said, "We must fulfill all righteousness."

92. Those who say they shall die and then arise are confused. If you do not receive the resurrection while you are alive you

will not receive anything when you die. This is why it is said that Baptism is great, because those who receive it shall live.

93. Philip the Apostle said, "Joseph the Carpenter planted a grove of trees because he needed wood for his work (craft or trade). He himself made the cross from the trees that he had planted, and his heir hung on that which he had planted. His heir was Jesus, and the tree was the cross. But the tree of life in the midst of the garden (paradise) is the olive tree. From the heart of it comes the anointing through the olive oil and from that comes the resurrection."

94. This world consumes corpses. Everything eaten by (in) the world dies. The truth devours life, but if you eat truth you shall never die. Jesus came (from there) bringing food. And to those wishing it (whom he wished) he gave life, so that they not die.

95. God created the garden (paradise). Man lived there, but they did not have God in their hearts and so they gave in to desire. This garden is where they will be said to us, " You may eat this but not eat that, according to your desire." This is the place where I shall choose to eat various things there such as the tree of knowledge, which slew Adam. In this

place the tree of knowledge gave life to man. The Torah is the tree. It has the power to impart the knowledge of good and evil. It did not remove him from the evil or deliver him to good. It simply caused those who had eaten it to die. Death began because truth said, " You can eat this, but do not eat that." This was the beginning of death.

96. The anointing (chrism) is made superior to Baptism, because from the word Chrism we are called Christians (Christ's ones / anointed ones) not because of the word Baptism. And because of Chrism he was called Christ. The Father anointed the Son, and the Son anointed the Apostles, and the Apostles anointed us. He who has been anointed has come to possess all things; he has the resurrection, the light, the cross, and the Holy Spirit. The Father bestowed this upon him in the Bridal-Chamber. The father gave it to the Son who received it freely. The Father was in the Son, and the Son was in the Father. This is the kingdom of Heaven.

97. It was perfectly said by the Lord: Some have attained the kingdom of Heaven laughing. They came forth from the world joyous. Those who belong to Christ who went down into the water immediately came up as lord of everything. He did not laugh because he took things lightly, but because he

saw that everything in this world was worthless compared to the kingdom of Heaven. If he scoffs at the world and sees its worthlessness he will come forth laughing.

98. Compared to the Bread and cup, and the oil of anointing (Chrism); there is another one superior to them all.

99. The world (system) began through a mistake. He who made this world wished to make it perfect and eternal. He failed (fell away / did not follow through) and did not attain his goal. The world is not eternal, but the children of the world are eternal. They were children and obtained eternity. No one can receive eternity except by becoming a child. The more you are unable to receive, the more you will be unable to give.

100. The cup of the communion (prayer) contains wine and water. It is presented as the symbol of the blood. Over it (because of the blood) we give thanks. It is filled by (with) the Holy Spirit. It (the blood) belongs to the Perfect Man. When we drink we consume the Perfect man.

101. The Living Water is a body. It is right that we be clothed with a living body (The Living Man). When he goes down

into the water he undresses himself so he may be clothed with the living man.

102. A horse naturally gives birth to a horse, a human naturally gives birth to a human, a god naturally gives birth to a god. The Bridegroom within the Bride gives birth to children who are born in the Bridal-Chamber. The Jews do not spring forth from Greeks (Gentiles), and Christians (those belonging to Christ) do not come from Jews. These who gave birth to Christians were called the chosen generation of the Holy Spirit (living God). The True Man, the Son of Mankind, was the seed that brought forth the sons of Man. This generation is the true ones in the world. This is the place where the children of the Bridal-Chamber dwell.

103. Copulation occurs in this world when man and woman mix (mingle or entwine). Strength joins with weakness. In eternity there is a different kind of mingling that occurs. Metaphorically we call it by the same names, but it is exalted beyond any name we may give it. It transcends brute strength. Where there is no force, there are those who are superior to force. Man cannot comprehend this.

104. The one is not, and the other one is, but they are united. This is He who shall not be able to come unto those who have a heart of flesh. (He is not here, but He exists. However, He cannot inhabit a heart of those who are attached to the fleshly world.)

105. Before you possess all knowledge, should you not know yourself? If you do not know yourself, how can you enjoy those things you have? Only those who have understood themselves shall enjoy the things they have come to possess.

106. The perfected person cannot be captured or seen. If they (Archons) could see him, they could capture him. The path to grace can only come from the perfect light. Unless one is clothed in the perfect light and it shows on and in him he shall not be able to come out from the World as the perfected son of the Bridal-Chamber. We must be perfected before we come out from the world. Whoever has received all before mastering all, will not be able to master the kingdom. He shall go to the transition (death) imperfect. Only Jesus knows his destiny.

107. The holy person (priest) is entirely holy, including his body. If one blesses the bread and sanctifies it, or the cup, or

everything else he receives, why will he not sanctify the body also?

108. By perfecting the water of Baptism: thus Jesus washed away death (removed death from it). Because of this, we are descended into the water but not into death. We are not poured out into the wind (spirit) of the world. Whenever that blows, its winter has come. When the Holy Spirit breathes, summer has come.

109. Whoever recognizes the truth is set free. He who is set free does not go back (sin), for the one who goes back (the sinner) is the slave of sin. Truth is the Mother. When we unite with her it is recognition of the truth. Those who are set free from sin (no longer have to sin) are called free by the world. It is the recognition of the truth that exalts the hearts of those who are set free from sin. This is what liberates them and places them over the entire world. Love builds (inspires). He who has been set free through this recognition is a slave of love, serving those who have not yet been set free by the truth. Knowledge makes them capable of being set free. Love does not take anything selfishly. How can it when it possesses all things? It does not say; "This is mine or that is mine," but it says, "All of this belongs to you."

110. Spiritual love is wine with fragrance. All those who are anointed with it enjoy it. Those who anoint themselves with it (are near to the anointed ones) enjoy it also. But when the anointed ones depart the bystanders who are not anointed remain in their own stench. The Samaritan gave nothing to the wounded man except wine and oil for anointing. The wounds were healed, for "love covers a multitude of sins."

111. The children of a woman resemble the man who loves her. If the man is her husband, they resemble her husband. If the man is her illicit lover, they resemble him. Often, a woman will have sex with her husband out of duty but her heart is with her lover with whom she also has sex. The children of such a union often resemble the lover. You who live with the Son of God and do not also love the world but love the Lord only will have children that look like the Lord and not the world.

112. Humans mate with the humans, horses mate with horses, donkeys mate with donkeys. Like attracts like and they group together. Spirits unite with Spirits, and the thought (Word) mingles with the thought (Word), as Light merges with Light. If you become a person then people will love you. If you

become a spirit, then the Spirit shall merge with you. If you become a thought (the Word), then the thought (the Word) shall unite with you. If you become enlightened, then the Light shall merge with you. If you rise above this world, then that which is from above shall rest upon (in) you. But, if you become like a horse, donkey, bull, dog, sheep, or any other animal, domestic or feral, then neither man nor Spirit nor Word (thought) nor the Light nor those from above nor those dwelling within shall be able to love you. They shall not be able to rest in you, and they will have no part in your inheritance to come.

113. He who is enslaved without his consent can be set free. He who has been set free by the grace of his master, but then sells himself back into slavery cannot be set free.

114. The cultivation in this world comes through four elements (earth, air, fire, water). Crops are harvested and taken into the barn only if there is first soil, water, wind, and light. God's harvest is also by means of four elements; faith (trust), hope (expectation), love (agape'), and knowledge (recognition of the truth). Our soil is the faith in which we take root. Our water is the hope by which we are nourished. Wind (spirit) is the love through which we grow. Light is the

truth, which causes us to ripen. But, it is Grace that causes us to become kings of all heaven. Their souls are among the blessed for they live in Truth.

115. Jesus, the Christ, came to all of us but did not lay any burden on us. This kind of person is perfect and blessed. He is the Word of God. Ask us about him and we will tell you his righteousness is difficult to define or describe. A task so great assures failure.

116. How will he give rest to everyone; great or small, believer or not? He provides rest to all. There are those who attempt to gain by assisting the rich. Those who see themselves as rich are picky. They do not come of their own accord. Do not grieve them or anyone. It is natural to want to do good, but understand that the rich may seek to cause grief and he who seeks to do good could annoy those who think they are rich.

117. A householder had acquired everything. He had children, slaves, cattle, dogs, and pigs. He also had wheat, barley, straw, hay, meat, oil, and acorns. He was wise and knew what each needed to eat. He fed his children bread and meat. He fed the slaves oil with grain. The cattle were given

barley, straw and hay. The dogs received bones and the pigs got acorns and bread scraps. This is how it is with the disciple of God. If he is wise, he understands discipleship. The bodily forms will not deceive him, but he will understand the condition of the souls around him. He will speak to each man on his own level. In the world there are many types of animals in human form. He must recognize each one. If the person is a pig, feed him acorns. If the person is a bull, feed him barley with straw and hay; if a dog, throw him bones. If a person is a slave feed him basic food, but to the sons present the perfect and complete food.

118. There is the Son of Man and there is the son of the son of Man. The Lord is the Son of Man, and his son creates through him. God gave the Son of Man the power to create; he also gave him the ability to have children. That which is created is a creature. Those born are a progeny (child or heir). A creature cannot propagate, but children can create. Yet they say that the creature procreates, however, the child is a creature. Therefore the creature's progeny are not his sons, but rather they are creations. He who creates works openly, and is visible. He who procreates does so in secret, and he hides himself from others. He who creates does so in open sight. He who procreates, makes his children (son) in secret.

119. No one is able to know what day a husband and wife copulate. Only they know, because marriage in this world is a sacrament (mystery) for those who have taken a wife. If the act of an impure (common) marriage is hidden, the pure (immaculate) marriage is a deeper mystery (sacrament) and is hidden even more. It is not carnal (common) but it is pure (undefiled). It is not founded on lust. It is founded on true love (agape'). It is not part of the darkness or night. It is part of the light. A marriage (act) which is seen (revealed or exposed) becomes vulgarity (common or prostitution), and the bride has played the whore not only if she has sex with another man, but also if she escapes from the Bridal-Chamber and is seen. She may only be seen (reveal herself to) by her father, her mother, the attendant (friend) of the bridegroom, and the bridegroom. Only these have permission to go into the bridal-chamber on a daily basis. Others will yearn to hear her voice or enjoy her perfume (fragrance of the anointing oil). Let them be fed like dogs from the scraps that fall from the table. Only those being from the Bridegroom belong with the Bride in the Bridal-Chamber. No one will be able to see the Bridegroom or the Bride unless he becomes one like (with) them.

120. When Abraham was allowed (rejoiced at seeing what he was) to see (the truth), he circumcised the flesh of the foreskin to show us that it was correct (necessary) to renounce (kill) the flesh of this world.

121. As long as the entrails of a person are contained, the person lives and is well. If his entrails are exposed and he is disemboweled, the person will die. It is the same with a tree. If its roots are covered it will live and grow, but if its roots are exposed the tree will wither and die. It is the same with everything born into this world. It is this way with everything manifest (seen) and covert (unseen). As long as the roots of evil are hidden, it is strong, but once evil is exposed or recognized it is destroyed and it dies. This is why the Word says; "Already the ax has been laid to the root of the tree." It will not only chop down the tree, because that will permit it to sprout again, the ax will go down into the ground and cleave the very root. Jesus uprooted what others had only partially cut down. Let each one of us dig deeply, down to the root of the evil that is within his heart and rip it out by its roots. If we can just recognize evil we can uproot it. However, if evil remains unrecognized, it will take root within us and yield its fruit in our hearts. It will make evil our master and we will be its slaves. Evil takes us captive, and coerces us into

doing what we do not want to do. Evil compels us into not doing what we should do. While it is unrecognized, it drives us .

122. Ignorance is the mother of all evil. Evil ends in confusion and death. Truth is like ignorance. If it is hidden it rests within itself, but when it is revealed it is recognized and it is stronger than ignorance and error. Truth wins and liberates us from confusion. The Word said; "You shall know the truth and the truth shall set you free." Ignorance seeks to make us its slaves but knowledge is freedom. By recognizing the truth, we shall find the fruits of the truth within our hearts. If we join ourselves with the truth we shall be fulfilled.

123. Now, we have the visible (beings) things of creation and we say that visible things (beings) are the powerful and honorable, but the invisible things are the weak and unworthy of our attention. The nature of truth is different. In it, the visible things (beings) are weak and lowly, but the invisible are the powerful and honorable. The wisdom of the invisible God cannot be made known to us except that he takes visible form in ways we are accustomed to. Yet the mysteries of the truth are revealed, in types and symbols, but the Bridal-Chamber is hidden as it is with the Holy of Holies.

124. The veil of the Temple first concealed how God governed creation. Once the veil was torn and the things within (the Holy of Holies) were revealed, the house was to be forsaken, abandoned, and destroyed. Yet the entire Divinity (Godhead) was to depart, not to the holies of the holies, for it was not able to merge with the light nor unite with the complete fullness. It was to be under the wings of the cross, in its open arms. This is the ark which shall be salvation for us when the destruction of water has overwhelmed (overtaken) them.

125. Those in the priestly tribe shall be able to enter within the veil of the Temple along with the High Priest. This was symbolized by the fact that the veil was not torn at the top only, (but was torn from top to the bottom). If it was torn only at the top it would have been opened only for those who are on high (from the higher realm). If it was torn at the bottom only it would have been revealed only to those who are from below (the lower realm). But it was torn from the top to the bottom. Those who are from above made it available to us who are below them, so that we might enter into the secret of the truth. This strengthening of us is most wonderful. Because of this, we can enter in by means of symbols even

though they are weak and worthless. They are humble and incomplete when compared to the perfect glory. It is the glory of glories and the power of powers. Through it the perfect is opened to us and it contains the secrets of the truth. Moreover, the Holies of Holies have been revealed and opened, and the Bridal-Chamber has invited us in.

126. As long as evil is hidden, and not completely purged from among the children of the Holy Spirit, it remains a potential threat. The children can be enslaved by the adversary, but when the Perfect Light is seen, it will pour out the oil of anointing upon and within it, and the slaves shall be set free and the slaves shall be bought back.

127. Every plant not sown by my heavenly Father shall be pulled up by the root. Those who were estranged shall be united and the empty shall be filled.

128. Everyone who enters the bridal-chamber shall ignite (be born in) the Light. This is like a marriage, which takes place at night. The fire is ablaze and is seen in the dark but goes out before morning. The mysteries (sacraments) of the marriage are consummated in the light of day, and that light never dies.

129. If someone becomes a child of the Bridal-Chamber, he shall receive the Light. If one does not receive it in this place, he will not be able to receive it in any other place. He who has received that Light shall not be seen, nor captured. No one in the world will be able to disturb him. When he leaves the world he will have already received the truth in types and symbols. The world has become eternity, because for him the fullness is eternal. It is revealed only to this kind of person. Truth is not hidden in darkness or the night. Truth is hidden in a perfect day and a holy light.

History of The Gospel Of Mary Magdalene

While traveling and researching in Cairo in 1896, German scholar, Dr. Carl Reinhardt, acquired a papyrus containing Coptic texts entitled the Revelation of John, the Wisdom of Jesus Christ, and the Gospel of Mary.

Before setting about to translate his exciting find, two world wars ensued, delaying publication until 1955. By then the Nag Hammadi collection had also been discovered.

Two of the texts in his codex, the Revelation of John, and the Wisdom of Jesus Christ, were included there. Importantly, the codex preserves the most complete surviving copy of the Gospel of Mary, named for its supposed author, Mary of Magdala. Two other fragments of the Gospel of Mary written in Greek were later unearthed in archaeological digs at Oxyrhynchus in Northern Egypt.

All of the various fragments were brought together to form the translation presented here. However, even with all of the fragments assembled, the manuscript of the Gospel of Mary is missing pages 1 to 6 and pages 11 to 14. These pages included sections of the text up to chapter 4, and portions of chapter 5 to 8.

Although the text of the Gospel of Mary is incomplete, the text presented below serves to shake the very concept of our assumptions of early Christianity as well as Christ's possible relationship to Mary of Magdala, whom we call Mary Magdalene.

The Gospel of Mary Magdalene

(Pages 1 to 6, containing chapters 1 - 3, could not be recovered.
The text starts on page 7, chapter 4)

Chapter 4

21) (And they asked Jesus), "Will matter then be destroyed or
not?"

22) The Savior said, "All nature, all things formed, and all
creatures exist in and with one another, and they will be
dissolved again into their own elements (origins).

23) This is because it is the nature of matter to return to its
original elements.

24) If you have an ear to hear, listen to this."

25) Peter said to him, "Since you have explained all things to
us, tell us this also: What sin did the world commit (what sin
is in the world)?"

26) The Savior said, "There is no sin (of the world). Each person makes his own sin when he does things like adultery (in the same nature as adultery). This is called sin.

27) That is why the Good came to be among you. He came to restore every nature to its basic root."

28) Then He continued; "You become sick and die because you did not have access to (knowledge of) Him who can heal you.

29) If you have any sense, you must understand this.

30) The material world produced a great passion (desire or suffering) without equal. This was contrary to the natural balance. The entire cosmos (body) was disturbed by it.

31) That is why I said to you, Be encouraged, and if you are discouraged be encouraged when you see the different forms nature has taken.

32) He who has ears to hear, let him hear."

33) When the Blessed One had said this, He greeted all of them and said; "Peace be with you. Take my peace into you.

34) Beware that no one deceives you by saying, 'Look (he is) here or look (he is) there. The Son of Man is within you.'

35) Follow Him there.

36) Those who seek Him will find Him.

37) Go now and preach the gospel (this good news) of the Kingdom.

38) Do not lay down any rules beyond what I told you, and do not give a law like the lawgivers (Pharisees) or you will be held to account for the same laws."

39) When He said this He departed.

Chapter 5

1) Then they were troubled and wept out loud, saying, "How shall we go to the Gentiles and preach the gospel of the

Kingdom of the Son of Man? If they did not spare Him, how can we expect that they will spare us?"

2) Then Mary stood up, greeted them all, and said to her fellow believers, "Do not weep and do not be troubled and do not waver, because His grace will be with you completely and it will protect you.

3) Instead, let us praise His greatness, because He has prepared us and made us into mature (finished or complete) people."

4) Mary's words turned their hearts to the Good, and they began to discuss the words of the Savior.

5) Peter said to Mary, "Sister we know that the Savior loved you more than all other women.

6) Tell us the words of the Savior that you remember and know, but we have not heard and do not know."

7) Mary answered him and said, "I will tell you what He hid from you."

8) And she began to speak these words to them: She said, "I saw the Lord in a vision and I said to Him, 'Lord I saw you today in a vision.'

9) He answered and said to me; 'You will be happy that you did not waver at the sight of Me. Where the mind is there is the treasure.'

10) I said to Him; 'Lord, does one see visions through the soul or through the spirit?'

11) The Savior answered and said; 'He sees visions through neither the soul nor the spirit. It is through the mind that is between the two. That is what sees the vision and it is (there the vision exists).'"

(Pages 11 - 14 are missing. Text begins again at chapter 8)

Chapter 8

10) And Desire, (a lesser god), said, "Before, I did not see you descending, but now I see you ascending. Why do you lie since you belong to me?"

11) The soul answered and said, "I saw you but you did not see me nor recognize me. I covered you like a garment and you did not know me."

12) When it said this, the soul went away greatly rejoicing.

13) Again it came to the third power (lesser god), which is called Ignorance.

14) The power questioned the soul, saying, "Where are you going? You are enslaved (captured) in wickedness. Since you are its captive you cannot judge (have no judgment)."

15) And the soul said, "Why do you judge me, when I have not judged?"

16) "I was captured, although I have not captured anyone."

17) "I was not recognized. But I have recognized that God (the All) is in (being dissolved) both the earthly things and in the heavenly (things)."

18) When the soul had overcome the third power, it ascended and saw the fourth power, which took seven forms.

19) The first form is darkness, the second desire, the third ignorance, the fourth is the lust of death, the fifth is the dominion of the flesh, the sixth is the empty useless wisdom of flesh, the seventh is the wisdom of vengeance and anger. These are the seven powers of wrath.

20) They asked the soul, "Where do you come from, slayer of men: where are you going, conqueror of space?"

21) The soul answered and said, "What has trapped me has been slain, and what kept me caged has been overcome."

22) "My desire has been ended, and ignorance has died."

23) "In an age (dispensation) I was released from the world in a symbolic image, and I was released from the chains of oblivion, which were only temporary (in this transient world)."

24) "From this time on will, I will attain the rest of the ages and seasons of silence."

Chapter 9

1) When Mary had said this, she fell silent, since she had shared all the Savior had told her.

2) But Andrew said to the other believers, "Say what you want about what she has said, but I do not believe that the Savior said this. These teachings are very strange ideas."

3) Peter answered him and spoke concerning these things.

4) He questioned them about the Savior and asked, "Did He really speak privately with a woman and not openly to us? Are we to turn around and all listen to her? Did He prefer her to us?"

5) Then Mary sobbed and said to Peter, "My brother Peter, what do you think? Do you think that I have made all of this up in my heart by myself? Do you think that I am lying about the Savior?"

6) Levi said to Peter, "Peter you have always had a hot temper.

7) Now I see you fighting against this woman like she was your enemy."

8) If the Savior made her worthy, who are you to reject her? What do you think you are doing? Surely the Savior knows her well?

9) That is why He loved her more than us. Let us be ashamed of this and let us put on the perfect Man. Let us separate from each other as He commanded us to do so we can preach the gospel, not laying down any other rule or other law beyond what the Savior told us."

10) And when they heard this they began to go out and proclaim and preach.

History of The Apocryphon of John

The Apocryphon, or "Secrets" of John forms the cornerstone of Gnostic mythology and cosmology. In this text we are introduced to the major entities of creation and lordship. We learn how the universe, including earth and man, came into being. The origin of evil, the creator god, and the material world are explained in detail. The story seems to be a mixture of various belief systems, including those of Plato, who seems to have borrowed freely from the format of Greek mythology, and Christianity. The story is loosely based on Genesis chapters 1 through 13 as a timeline.

The basic text of the Apocryphon of John existed in some form before 185 C.E. when a book called the Apocryphon of John was referred to by Irenaeus in his book, Against Heresies (Adversus Haereses), written in that year. Irenaeus reported about the Gnostic texts saying that teachers in 2nd century Christian communities were writing their own books to gain converts. He called these books, "an indescribable number of secret and illegitimate writings, which they themselves have forged, to bewilder the minds of foolish people, who are ignorant of the true scriptures" (A.H. 1.20.1)

The Apocryphon of John continued to be circulated, expanded, and embellished for the next seven hundred years. The document was reportedly in use during the eighth century by the Audians of Mesopotamia.

Part of the mythology revealed in the Apocryphon of John is also present in the Gnostic book, The Sophia (Wisdom) of Jesus as well as other Gnostic texts.

The specific document that so angered Irenaeus was lost and remained so until 1945, when a library of papyrus codices from the 4th century A.D. were found at Nag Hammadi in Egypt. The Apocryphon of John was among the texts,

Four versions have been found thus far. These are comprised of a long version, of which we have two identical Coptic manuscripts. A short version is also Coptic but differs from the others by eliminating certain details. Among the texts, a third manuscript had been found that differs slightly from the first shorter manuscript in style and vocabulary. A fragment has been found that shows some minor differences which distinguish it from the other.

Which, if any, of these texts are original has not been determined, however, it is the longer version that is presented here. This version was chosen because it contained more details and offered an overall cohesion of thought. This could be due to additions and embellishments sown through the shorter, less detailed versions.

Since we have already covered the general idea behind Gnostic mythology it need not be repeated here. However, a chart showing the main characters and their position on the divine family tree might serve us well. It is shown below.

Simplified Cast Of Characters

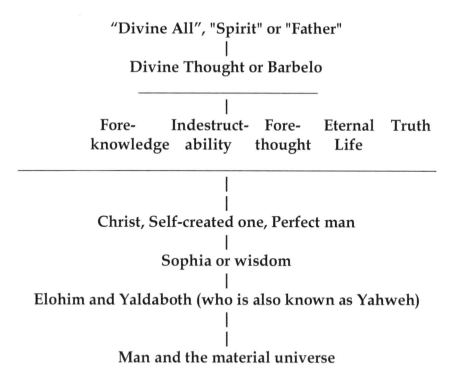

"Divine All", "Spirit" or "Father"
|
Divine Thought or Barbelo
_____

|

| Fore-knowledge | Indestruct-ability | Fore-thought | Eternal Life | Truth |

|
|
Christ, Self-created one, Perfect man
|
Sophia or wisdom
|
Elohim and Yaldaboth (who is also known as Yahweh)
|
|
Man and the material universe

The Apocryphon of John

The teaching of the savior, that will reveal the mysteries of things hidden which he taught John, his disciple, in silence. On the day when John, the brother of James, the sons of Zebedee, had come to the temple, a Pharisee named Arimanius came up to him and said, Where is your master whom you followed? He said to him, He has gone back to the place he came from. The Pharisee said to him, This Nazarene deceived all of you with his deception. He filled your ears with lies, and closed your hearts and turned you all away from your fathers' traditions.

When I, John, heard these things I walked away from the temple into the desert. I grieved greatly in my heart, saying, How was the savior appointed, and why was he sent to the world by his Father, and who is his Father who sent him, and to which kingdom shall we go? What did he mean when he said to us, This kingdom which you will go to is an imperishable kingdom, but he did not teach us what kind it is.

Then, while I was meditating on these things, I saw the heavens open and the whole creation below heaven was shining and the world shook. I was afraid, and then I saw in the light a young man who stood by me. As I was looking at him he became like an old man. And he changed his visage again and become like a servant. There were not many beings in front of me, but there was a single being with many forms composed of light, and they could be seen through each other, and there were three forms within the one being.

He said to me, John, John, why do you doubt, and why are you afraid? (Mat. 28:17) Do you understand this image, do you not? Do not be afraid! I am the one who is with all of you always. I am the Father and the Mother, and I am the Son. I am the undefiled and incorruptible one. I have come to teach you what is and what was and what will be, so that you may know the things visible and invisible, and to teach you concerning the upright, immutable (unshakable/ unwavering) race of the perfect Man. Now, therefore, lift up your face, that you may receive the things that I shall teach you today, and may tell them to your fellow spirits who are from the upright, immutable (unwavering/ unshakable) race of the perfect Man. (Eph.4:13)

And I asked if I might understand it, and he said to me, The

One God is a king with nothing above it. It is he who exists as God and Father of everything, the invisible One who rules over everything, who exists as incorruptible, which is in the pure light that no eye can look upon.

He is the invisible Spirit. It is not correct to think of him as a god, or anything similar. He is more than god, since there is nothing above him, for no one is above him. He does not exist within anything inferior to him, because everything exists within him. He has established himself. He is eternal, self-sufficient, and self-sustaining. He is complete perfection. He did not lack anything to be complete and he is continually perfect in light. He is unlimited, since there was no one before him to limit him. He is unknowable, since there exists no one prior to him to comprehend him. He is immeasurable, since there was no one before him to measure him. He is invisible, since no one has seen him. He is eternal, since he exists always. He is an enigma, since no one was able to apprehend him or explain him. He is unnamable, since there is no one who came before him to give him a name.

He is One, immeasurable light, which is pure, holy and immaculate. He is too sacred to speak of, being perfect and incorruptible. He is beyond perfection, blessedness, and divinity, because he is vastly superior to them all. He is not corporeal nor is he incorporeal. He is One and cannot be qualified or quantified, for no one can know him. He is not one among other beings; instead, he is far superior to all. He is so superior to all things that his essence is not part of the kingdoms, nor is he part of time. He who is a kingdom was created beforehand. Time does not matter to him, since he does not receive anything from another, for it would be received on loan. He who comes first needs nothing from anyone. Such a one expectantly beholds himself in his own light. He is majestic perfection. He is pure, immeasurable mind. He is a kingdom that gives the kingdoms their kingdom. He is life that gives life. He is the blessed One that blesses. He is knowledge and he gives knowledge. He is goodness that gives goodness. He is mercy and redemption and he bestows mercy. He is grace that gives grace. He does not give because he has these things but he gives the immeasurable, incomprehensible light from which all things flow.

How am I to speak with you about him? His kingdom is indestructible, at peace and existing in silence, at rest before everything was. He is the head of all the kingdoms (kingdoms), and he gives them strength in his goodness. For we know not the things that are unspeakably sacred, and we do not understand that which cannot be measured, except for him who was created from him, namely from the Father. It is he alone who told it to us.

He who beholds himself in the light which surrounds him and comes from him is the spring of the water of life. It is he who sustains the entire kingdom in every way, and it is he who gazes upon the image which he sees in the spring of the Spirit. It is he who puts his desire in the liquid light which is in the spring of the pure liquid light which surrounds him. The Father's thought performed a deed and she was created from it. It is she who had appeared before him in the shining of his light. This is the first power which was before all of them and which was created from his mind. She is the Thought of the All and her light shines like his light. It is the perfect power which is the visage of the invisible. She is the pure, undefiled Spirit who is perfect. She is the first power, the glory of Barbelo, the perfect glory of the kingdom (kingdoms), the glory revealed. She glorified the pure, undefiled Spirit and it was she who praised him, because thanks to him she had come forth. She is the first thought, his image; she became the womb of everything, for it is she who preceded them all. She is the Mother-Father, the first man, the Holy Spirit, the threefold male, the triple power, the androgynous one with three names, and the eternal kingdom among the invisible ones, and the first to come forth.

She asked the invisible, pure, undefiled Spirit, Barbelo, to give her Foreknowledge, and the Spirit agreed. And when he had agreed, the Foreknowledge was created, and it stood by the Thought; it originates from the thought of the invisible, pure, undefiled Spirit. Foreknowledge glorified him and his perfect power, Barbelo. It was because of her that Foreknowledge had been created.

And she asked again to grant her indestructibility, and he agreed. When he had agreed, indestructibility was created, and it stood by the Divine Thought and the Foreknowledge. It glorified the invisible One and Barbelo, because of whom it had been created.

And Barbelo asked to grant her Eternal Life. And the invisible Spirit agreed. And when he had agreed, Eternal Life was created, and they attended and glorified the invisible Spirit and Barbelo, the one because of whom they had been created.

And she asked again to grant her truth. And the invisible Spirit agreed. And when he had agreed, Truth was created, and they attended and glorified the invisible, excellent Spirit and his Barbelo, the one because of whom they had been created.

This is the five-fold creation of the kingdom of the Father, which is the first man and the image of the invisible Spirit, which came from Barbelo, who was the divine Thought; Forethought, Foreknowledge, Indestructibility, Eternal life, and Truth.

This is the androgynous five-fold being of the kingdom, which is the ten types of kingdoms, which is the Father. (Five, being both male and female, or neither male nor female, become ten.)

And he looked at Barbelo with his pure light which surrounds the invisible Spirit, and his sparks, and she was impregnated by him. And a spark of light produced a light resembling his blessedness but it did not equal his greatness. This was the only-begotten child of the Mother-Father which had come forth. It is the only offspring and the only begotten of the Father, the pure Light.

And the invisible, pure, undefiled Spirit rejoiced over the light which was created, that which was produced by the first power of his Thought, which is Barbelo. And he poured his goodness over it until it became perfect and did not lack in any goodness, because he had anointed the child with the goodness of the invisible Spirit. It was his child and the child was there with him and he poured upon the child an anointing. And immediately when the child had received the Spirit, it glorified the Holy Spirit and the perfect Divine Thought, because the child owed these its existence.

And it asked to be given Mind as a fellow worker, and he agreed gladly. And when the invisible Spirit had agreed, the Mind was created, and it attended the anointed one (Christ), glorifying him and Barbelo. And all these were created in silence.

And Mind wanted to initiate an action through the word of the invisible Spirit. Thus, his will became an action and it appeared with the mind; and the light glorified it. And the word followed the will. It was because of the word that Christ, the divine self-created one, created everything. And Eternal Life and his will and Mind and Foreknowledge attended and glorified the invisible Spirit and Barbelo, because of whom they had been created.

And the Holy Spirit perfected and matured the divine Self-created one, and brought the son, together with Barbelo, so that he might present himself to the mighty and invisible, pure, undefiled Spirit as the divine Self-created one, the Christ (the anointed one) who loudly proclaimed honor to the spirit. He was created through Forethought. And the invisible, pure, undefiled Spirit placed the divine Self-created one of truth over everything. And he caused every authority to be subject to him and to Truth, which is in him, so that he may know the name of the "All," whose name is exalted above every name. That name will only be spoken to those who are worthy of it.

From the light, which is the Christ, there is incorruptibleness and through the gift of the Spirit four lights shone from the divine Self-created one. He wished that they might be with him. And the three are will, thought, and life. And the four powers are Understanding, Grace, Perception, and Thoughtfulness.

And Grace belongs to the everlasting realm of the luminary Harmozel, which is the first angel. And there are three other kingdoms with this everlasting kingdom: Grace, Truth, and Form. And the second luminary is Oriel, who has authority over the second everlasting realm. And there are three other kingdoms with him: Conception, Perception, and Memory. And the third luminary is Daveithai, who has authority over the third everlasting realm. And there are three other kingdoms with him: Understanding, Love, and Idea. And the fourth luminary, Eleleth , was given authority over the fourth everlasting realm. And there are three other kingdoms with him: Perfection, Peace, and Wisdom (Sophia). These are the four luminaries which serve the divine Self-created one. These are the twelve kingdoms which serve the child of god, the Self-created one, the Christ. They serve him through the will and the grace of the invisible Spirit. The twelve kingdoms belong to the child of the Self-created one. All things were established by the will of the Holy Spirit through the Self-created one.

From the Foreknowledge of the perfect mind, through the expression of the will of the invisible Spirit and the will of the Self-created one, the perfect Man came into being. He was the first revelation and the truth. The pure, undefiled Spirit called him "Adam, The Stranger" (not of the earthly realm, but belonging to the divine realm). The spirit placed him over the first realm with the mighty one, the Self-created one, the Christ, by the authority of the first luminary, Harmozel; and with him are his powers. And the invisible one gave Adam The Stranger an invincible spiritual power. And Adam The Stranger spoke, glorifying and praising the invisible Spirit, saying, "It is because of you that everything has been created and therefore, everything will return to you. I shall praise and glorify you and the Self-created one and all the realms, the three: the Father, the Mother, and the Son, who make up the perfect power."

And Adam The Stranger placed his son Seth over the second realm in which the second luminary Oriel is present. And in the third realm the children of Seth were established over the third luminary, Daveithai. And the souls of the saints were lodged there. In the fourth realm the souls are kept of those who do not know the pleroma and who did not repent at once. These are they who persisted for a while and repented afterwards; they are in the area of the fourth luminary, Eleleth. They are those which glorify the invisible Spirit.

And the Sophia of the eternal realm manifested a thought from herself through the invisible Spirit and Foreknowledge. She wanted to produce a likeness of herself out of herself without the consent of the Spirit, but he had not approved. She attempted this act without her male consort, and without his permission. She had no male approval thus, she had not found her agreement. She had considered this without the consent of the Spirit and the knowledge of her compliment, but she brought forth her creation anyway. Because of the invincible power she possessed her thought did not remain idle, and something came out of her which was imperfect and different from her appearance because she had produced it without her compliment. It did not look like its mother because it has another form.

As she beheld the results of her desire, it changed into a form of a lion-faced serpent. Its eyes were like fire-like lightning which flashed. When she saw it she cast it away from her and threw it outside the realm so that none of the immortal ones might see it, for she had created it in ignorance. She surrounded it with a brightly glowing cloud and she put a throne in the middle of the cloud that no one might see it except the Holy Spirit who is called the mother of all that lives. And she called his name Yaldaboth.

This is the first Archon who took great power from his mother. And he left her and moved away from the realm in which he was born. He became strong and created for himself other kingdoms with a flame of glowing fire which still existed. And he mated with his own mindless ego that he had with him (he masturbated / or he was like his mother and did the same act of creation by himself) and brought into existence authorities for himself.

The name of the first one is Athoth, whom the generations call the reaper.

The second one is Harmas, who is the eye of envy.

The third one is Kalila-Oumbri.

The fourth one is Yabel.

The fifth one is Adonaiou, who is called Sabaoth (fool or chaos).

The sixth one is Cain, whom the generations of humans call the sun.

The seventh is Abel.

The eighth is Abrisene.

The ninth is Yobel.

The tenth is Armoupieel.

The eleventh is Melceir-Adonein.

The twelfth is Belias, it is he who is over the depth of Hades. (These could be the 12 stations of the zodiac.)

There he placed seven kings corresponding to the sections of heaven to reign over the seven heavens and he placed five to reign over the depth of the abyss. (There were 7 known planets at the time of writing.) And he shared his fire with them, but he did not relinquish any power of the light which he had taken from his mother, for he is ignorant darkness.

167

And when light is added to darkness, it made the darkness bright. When darkness is added to light, it dims the light and it became neither light nor dark, but it became like dusk.

Now the Archon who is like the gloaming (gloom) has three names. The first name is Yaldaboth (fool / son of chaos), the second is Saklas, and the third is Samael. And he is evil in the arrogance and thoughtlessness that is in him. For he said, "I am God and there is no other God beside me" (Isaiah chapters 45 and 46). He said this because he did not know where his strength originated, nor from where he himself had come.

And the Archons created seven powers for themselves, and the powers created for themselves six angels for each one until they became 365 angels (the number of days in the solar year). And these are the bodies belonging with the names:
The first is Athoth, a he has a sheep's face;
The second is Eloaiou, he has a donkey's face;
The third is Astaphaios, he has a hyena's face;
The fourth is Yao, he has a snake face with seven heads;
The fifth is Sabaoth, he has a dragon's face;
The sixth is Adonin, he has an ape face;
The seventh is Sabbede (or Sabbadaios), he has a face that

shone like fire.

This is the nature of seven types within the week.

But Yaldaboth had a plethora of faces, more than all of them, so that he could exhibit any face he wished to any of them, when he is in the midst of seraphim (seraphim plural of seraph. Seraphim are a class or type of angel of which, according to this text, Yaldaboth seems to be the head). He shared his fire with them and became their lord. He called himself God because of the power of the glory (brightness) he possessed that was taken from his mother's light. He rebelled against the place from which he came.

And he united the seven powers of his thoughts with the authorities that were with him. And when he spoke it became (happened).

And he named each power beginning with the highest:
The first is goodness with the first authority, Athoth;
The second is foreknowledge with the second power, Eloaio;
The third is divinity with the third one, Astraphaio);
The fourth is lordship with the fourth power, Yao;
The fifth is kingdom with the fifth one, Sabaoth;
The sixth is envy with the sixth one, Adonein;

The seventh is understanding with the seventh one, Sabbateon.

And these each has a kingdom (sphere on influence) within the realm (kingdom of heaven).

They were given names according to the glory belonging to heaven for the powers of their destructiveness. And there was power in the names given to them by their creator. But the names they were given according to the glory of heaven would mean their loss of power and their destruction. Thus they have two names.

He (Yaldaboth) created all things and structured things after the model of the first kingdom created so that he might create things in an incorruptible manner. It was not because he had ever seen the indestructible ones, but the power in him, which he had taken from his mother, produced in him the image of the order of the universe. And when he saw the creation surrounding him the innumerable amount of angels around him that had come from him, he said to them, "I am a jealous God, and there is no other God beside me." (Exodus 20:3) But by announcing this he had let the angels who were with him know that there is another God. If there were no other god, why would he be jealous?

Then the mother began to move here and there. She realized she has lost part of herself when the brightness of her light dimmed. And she became darker because her partner had not consorted with her.

I (John) said, Lord, what does it mean that she moved here and there? The lord smiled and said, "Do not think it happened the way that Moses said it did 'above the waters'." (Genesis 1:2) No, it did not, but when she had seen the wickedness which had happened, and the fact her son had stolen from her, she repented. In the darkness of ignorance she began to forget and to be ashamed. She did not dare to go back there, but she was restless. This restlessness was the moving here and there.

And the prideful one stole power from his mother. For he was ignorant and thought that there was no other in existence except his mother. When he saw innumerable angels he had created he exalted himself above them. When the mother recognized that the cloak (body) of darkness was imperfect, and she knew that her partner had not consorted with her, she repented and wept greatly. The entire pleroma heard the prayer of her repentance, and they praised the invisible, pure, undefiled Spirit on her behalf. And the Spirit agreed and when he agreed the Holy Spirit anointed her from the entire pleroma. For her consort did not come to her alone, but he brought to her through the pleroma that which was needed to restore what she was lacking. And she was allowed to ascend, not to her own kingdom but to the kingdom above her son, that she could remain in the ninth (heaven / kingdom) until she restored what she lacked in herself.

And a voice called from the highest kingdom of heaven: "The Man exists and the son of Man." And the head Archon, Yaldaboth, heard it and thought that the voice had come from his mother. He did not know whence it came. He taught them, the holy and perfect Mother-Father, the complete Foreknowledge, the image of the invisible one who is the Father of the all things and through whom everything came into being, the first Man. He is the one who revealed his image in human form.

And the whole kingdom of the first (head) Archon quaked, and the foundations of the abyss shook. And the underside of waters, which are above material world, were illuminated by the appearance of his image which had been revealed. When all the authorities and the head Archon looked, they saw the whole region of the underside (of the waters) that was illuminated. And through the light they saw the form of the image (reflected) in the water.

And he (Yaldaboth) said to the authorities of him, "Come, let us make a man using the image of God as a template to our likeness, that his image may become a light for us." And they created by the means of their various powers matching the features which were given to them. And each authority supplied a feature in the form of the image which Yaldaboth had seen in its natural form. He created a being according to the likeness of the first, perfect Man. And they said, "Let us call him Adam (man), that his name may be a power of light for us."

And the powers began to create.
The first one, Goodness, created a bone essence; and the second, Foreknowledge, created a sinew essence; the third, Divinity, created a flesh essence; and the fourth, the Lordship, created a marrow essence; the fifth, Kingdom created a blood essence; the sixth, Envy, created a skin essence; the seventh, Understanding, created a hair essence. And the multitude of the angels were with him and they received from the powers the seven elements of the natural (form) so they could create the proportions of the limbs and

173

the proportion of the buttocks and correct functioning of each of the parts together.

The first one began to create the head. Eteraphaope-Abron created his head; Meniggesstroeth created the brain; Asterechme created the right eye; Thaspomocha, the left eye; Yeronumos, the right ear; Bissoum, the left ear; Akioreim, the nose; Banen-Ephroum, the lips; Amen, the teeth; Ibikan, the molars; Basiliademe, the tonsils; Achcha, the uvula; Adaban, the neck; Chaaman, the vertebrae; Dearcho, the throat; Tebar, the right shoulder; the left shoulder; Mniarcon, the right elbow; the left elbow; Abitrion, the right underarm; Evanthen, the left underarm; Krys, the right hand; Beluai, the left hand; Treneu, the fingers of the right hand; Balbel, the fingers of the left hand; Kriman, the nails of the hands; Astrops, the right breast; Barroph, the left breast; Baoum, the right shoulder joint; Ararim, the left shoulder joint; Areche, the belly; Phthave, the navel; Senaphim, the abdomen; Arachethopi, the right ribs; Zabedo, the left ribs; Barias, the right hip; Phnouth the left hip; Abenlenarchei, the marrow; Chnoumeninorin, the bones; Gesole, the stomach; Agromauna, the heart; Bano, the lungs; Sostrapal, the liver; Anesimalar, the spleen; Thopithro, the intestines; Biblo, the kidneys; Roeror, the sinews; Taphreo, the spine of the body;

Ipouspoboba, the veins; Bineborin, the arteries; Atoimenpsephei, theirs are the breaths which are in all the limbs; Entholleia, all the flesh; Bedouk, the right buttock; Arabeei, the penis; Eilo, the testicles; Sorma, the genitals; Gorma-Kaiochlabar, the right thigh; Nebrith, the left thigh; Pserem, the kidneys of the right leg; Asaklas, the left kidney; Ormaoth, the right leg; Emenun, the left leg; Knyx, the right shin-bone; Tupelon, the left shin-bone; Achiel, the right knee; Phnene, the left knee; Phiouthrom, the right foot; Boabel, its toes; Trachoun, the left foot; Phikna, its toes; Miamai, the nails of the feet; Labernioum.

And those who were appointed over all of these are: Zathoth, Armas, Kalila, Jabel, (Sabaoth, Cain, Abel). And those who are particularly active in the limbs are the head Diolimodraza, the neck Yammeax, the right shoulder Yakouib, the left shoulder Verton, the right hand Oudidi, the left one Arbao, the fingers of the right hand Lampno, the fingers of the left hand Leekaphar, the right breast Barbar, the left breast Imae, the chest Pisandriaptes, the right shoulder joint Koade, the left shoulder joint Odeor, the right ribs Asphixix, the left ribs Synogchouta, the belly Arouph, the womb Sabalo, the right thigh Charcharb, the left thigh Chthaon, all the genitals Bathinoth, the right leg Choux, the left leg Charcha, the right shin-bone Aroer, the left shin-bone

175

Toechtha, the right knee Aol, the left knee Charaner, the right foot Bastan, its toes Archentechtha, the left foot Marephnounth, its toes Abrana.

Seven have power over all of these: Michael, Ouriel, Asmenedas, Saphasatoel, Aarmouriam, Richram, Amiorps. And the ones who are in charge of the senses are Archendekta; and he who is in charge of the receptions is Deitharbathas; and he who is in charge over the imagination is Oummaa; and he who is over creativity Aachiaram, and he who is over the whole impulse Riaramnacho.

The origin of the demons that are in the entire body is known to be these four: heat, cold, wetness, and dryness. And the mother of all of them is the material creation. And he who rules over the heat is Phloxopha; and he who rules over the cold is Oroorrothos; and he who rules over what is dry is Erimacho; and he who rules over the wetness is Athuro. And the mother of all of these is Onorthochrasaei, who stands in with them without limits, and she covorts with all of them. She is truly material and they are sustained by her.

The four ruling demons are: Ephememphi, who is attached to pleasure,

Yoko, who is attached to desire,

Nenentophni, who is attached to grief,

Blaomen, who is attached to fear,

and the mother of them all is Aesthesis-Ouch-Epi-Ptoe.

And from the four demons passions was created. And grief

spawned envy, jealousy, distress, trouble, pain, callousness,

anxiety, mourning, and more. Pleasure spawned wickedness,

vanity, pride, and similar things. Desire spawned anger,

wrath, and bitterness, and driving passion, the inability to be

satisfied, and similar things. Fear spawned dread,

subservience, agony, and shame. These are both good and

evil, but the understanding of their nature is attributed to

Anaro, who is over the material soul. It belongs with the

seven senses, which are controlled by Ouch-Epi-Ptoe.

This is the number of the angels: together they are 365. They

all worked on it from limb to limb, until the physical

(material) body was completed by them. Now there are other

ones in charge over the remaining passions whom I did not

mention to you. But if you wish to know them, it is written in

the book of Zoroaster. And all the angels and demons worked

until they had constructed (fashioned) the physical body.

And their creation was completely devoid of activity and was

motionless for a long time.

And when the mother (Sophia) wanted to recapture the power which was taken from her by the head Archon, she prayed to the Mother-Father of the All, who is most merciful. He sent a holy decree containing the five lights down to the place where the angels of the head Archon reside. They advised him (Yaldaboth) that he should bring forth the power of the mother. And they said to Yaldaboth, "Blow some of your spirit into his face and his body will arise." And he blew the spirit power of the mother into his (Adam's) face. (Genesis 2:7) Yaldaboth did not know to do this because he existed in ignorance. And the power of the mother went out of Yaldaboth into Adam's physical body, which they had fashioned after the image of the one who exists from the beginning. The body moved and gained strength, and it was enlightened.

And in that instant the other powers became jealous, although he (Adam) had been created through all of them. They were jealous because they had given Adam their power and now he was more intelligent than those who had made him, and his mind was greater than that of the head Archon. And when they recognized that he was enlightened, and that he could think better than they, and that he was free of evil, they took him and threw him into the lowest material realm.

But the blessed One, the Mother-Father, the giving and gracious One, had mercy on the power of the mother which had been transmitted from the head Archon because he did not want the Archons to gain power over the material body again. Therefore, he sent, a helper to Adam through his giving Spirit and his great compassion. The enlightened Thought which comes out of him is called "Life" (Zoe means life and is the name of Eve in certain Greek texts and the Septuagint). And she assists the whole creature, by working with him and restoring him to his fullness and by teaching him about the descent (flaws) of his seed and by teaching him about the way of ascent (to go upward again), which is based on the way he came down. (Rom. 8:22)

And the enlightened Thought was hidden within Adam so that the Archons would not know she was there, but that the Thought might restore (correct) what was lacking of the mother.

And the man was revealed because of the shadow of light in him. And his thinking was higher than all those who had made him. When they looked up they realized that his thinking was superior. Then they conspired with the entire force of Archons and angels. They took fire and earth and water as a mixture and added the four fiery winds. And they worked them together and caused a great noise. And they brought Adam into the shadow of death so that that they might re-make him from earth, water, fire and the spirit (wind) which make up matter. This was the ignorance of their darkness and desire, and their lying (false) spirit. This is the tomb of the re-formed body that the thieves had clothed Adam in. It contained the bonds of forgetfulness and cause him to become a mortal entity. He is the first one who came down, and the first to be separated (from the Divine All). Now, it is up to the Thought of the light which was in him to awaken his thinking.

And the Archons took him and placed him in paradise. And they said to him, "Eat at your leisure," (Genesis 2:16) for their pleasure is bitter and their beauty is twisted. Their pleasure is entrapment and their trees lack any holiness and their fruit is deadly poison and their promise is death. And the tree of their life they had placed in the center of paradise (Genesis 2:9).

And I (Jesus) shall teach all of you the mystery of their life. It is the plan that they made together, which is made from the template of their spirit. The root of this tree is bitter and its branches are death, its shadow is hate. Its leaves are a trap, and its blossom is the ointment of evil. Its fruit is death and its seed is desire. It sprouts (blooms) in darkness. Those who taste it dwell in Hades, and they rest in darkness.

But what they call "the tree of knowledge of good and evil" is the Thought of the light. They stationed themselves in front of it so that Adam might not understand his fullness and recognize his nakedness and be ashamed. But it was I (Jesus) who made them decide what they ate.

I said to the savior, Lord, wasn't it the serpent that instructed Adam to eat? The savior smiled and said, The serpent instructed them to eat because of its evil desire to produced sexual lust and destruction so that Adam would be useful to him. Adam knew that he was disobedient to Yaldaboth because the light of the Thought lived in him and made him stronger and more accurate in his thinking than the head Archon. Yaldaboth wanted to harvest the power that he himself had given Adam. And he caused Adam to forget.

And I said to the savior, "What is this forgetfulness?" He said, "It is not how Moses wrote and it is not how you have heard. He wrote in his first book, 'He put him to sleep' (Genesis 2:21), but that was how Adam perceived it. For also he said through the prophet, 'I will make their minds heavy, that they may not perceive nor understand.' (Isaiah 6:10)."

The Thought of the light hid herself in Adam. The head Archon wanted to bring her out through his rib but the Thought of the light cannot be apprehended. Although darkness pursued her, it did not catch her. Yaldaboth brought out part of Adam's power and he created another and formed a woman, using the template of the Thought which he had seen. The power he had taken from the Adam was formed into the female. This is what happened and not as Moses said, 'She was formed from the bone of his rib.' (Genesis 2:21)

Adam saw the woman beside him. In that instant the enlightened Thought appeared. She lifted the veil which occluded his mind. Adam sobered from the drunkenness of darkness and recognized his counterpart (compliment / agreement) , and he said, 'This is indeed bone of my bones and flesh of my flesh.' (Genesis 2:23) Therefore the man will leave his father and his mother, and he will cleave to his wife, and they will both be one flesh. (Genesis 2:24) For his partner will be sent to him and he will leave his father and his mother .

Our sister Sophia is the one who came down innocently in order to reclaim what she has lost. That is why she was called Life, because she is the mother of all things living, by the Foreknowledge of the sovereignty of heaven. Through her they that live have tasted the perfect Knowledge. I (Jesus) appeared in the form of an eagle on the tree of knowledge, which is the Thought from the Foreknowledge of the pure light. I did this so that I might teach them and wake them from them the deep sleep. For they were both in a fallen state, and they recognized they were naked. The Thought appeared to them in the form of light and she awakened their minds.

When Yaldaboth noticed that they fled from him, he cursed the earth he had made. He found the woman as she was preparing herself for her husband. He was lord over her, though he did not know the mystery was instated through the holy plan, so they were afraid to rebel against Yaldaboth. And he demonstrated to his angels the ignorance in him by casting them out of paradise, and he clothed them in darkening blackness.

And the head Archon, Yaldaboth, saw the virgin standing

beside Adam, but he was ignorant to the fact that the enlightened Thought of life had appeared in her. But when the Foreknowledge of All noticed it, she sent agents and they quickly stole the life (Zoe) out of Eve.

Then, the head Archon seduced her and he conceived two sons in her. The first is Eloim and the second is Yahweh. Eloim has a face like a bear and Yahweh has a face like a cat. The one is righteous but the other is unjust. (Yahweh is related to the New Testament and is considered a more just and kind God. Eloim is related to the Old Testament and is considered a jealous, revengeful, wrathful God.) He set Yahweh over fire and wind, and he set Eloim over water and earth. And he name them Cain and Abel in an attempt to deceive.

Sexual intercourse continues to this very day because of the head Archon. He instilled sexual desire in the woman who belongs to Adam. And Adam, through intercourse caused bodies to be replicated, and Yaldaboth breathed into them with his fraudulent spirit.

And he set the two Archons (Elohim and Yahweh) over principal elements, so that they might rule over the tomb (body). When Adam recognized the image of his own Foreknowledge, he begot the image of the son of man (Jesus) and he called him Seth, according to the fashion of the divine race living in the ethereal kingdoms. The mother (Sophia) sent her spirit also. It was in her image and was a replica of those who are in the pleroma. In this way she will prepare a dwelling place for the kingdoms to come.

Yaldaboth made them drink water of forgetfulness that he had made so that they might not remember from where they came. The seed remained with man for a while to assist him so that when the Spirit comes out from the holy kingdoms, he may raise up and heal him of his lack so the whole pleroma may again become holy and complete.

And I said to the savior, Lord, will all the souls be led safely into the pure light? He answered me and said, "Great things have arisen in your mind, and it is difficult to explain them to anyone except those from the race that cannot be moved. These are they on whom the Spirit of life will descend and with whom will be with the Power. They will be saved and become complete, perfect and worthy of greatness. They will be purified from all wickedness and evil actions. Then they will have no other care other than the incorruption, on which they shall focus their attention from here on, without anger or envy or jealousy or desire and greed for anything. They are affected by nothing except existing in the flesh, which they bear while looking expectantly for the time when they will be met by those who will receive them (their body). Such ones are worthy of the (incorruptible) imperishable, eternal life and the calling. They endure everything and bear up under everything, that they may finish the good fight (wrestling contest) and inherit eternal life. (Cor. 13:7)

I said to him, Lord, will the souls of those who did not do these works (things) but on whom the power and Spirit descended, be rejected? He answered and said to me, "If the Spirit descended upon them, they will certainly be saved, and they will be changed. The power will descend on every man, for without it no one could stand. And after they are born, when the Spirit of life grows in them and the power comes and strengthens that soul, no one can be led astray with evil deeds, but those on whom the false spirit falls are drawn astray by him.

I said, Lord, where will the souls go when they shed their flesh? And he laughed (smiled) and said to me, "The soul in which the power will become stronger than the false spirit is strong and she (the soul) turns and runs from evil and through the intervention of the incorruptible one, she is saved, taken up to the kingdoms and will rest there.

And I said, "Lord, what about those who do not know to whom they belong, where will their souls go?" And he said to me, "Those, the spoiled (double-minded) spirit has gained strength while they went astray and that casts a burden on the soul and draws her towards the deeds of evil, and he throws her down into forgetfulness. After she comes out of the body, it is handed over to the authorities that came into being through the Archon. They bind her with chains and cast her into prison, and hound her until she is set free from the forgetfulness and acquires knowledge. If she becomes perfected she is saved.

And I said, Lord, how can the soul become young again and return to its mother's womb or into (another) man? (This is a question regarding reincarnation.) He was glad when I asked him this, and he said to me, "You are blessed because you have understood!" That soul is made to follow another, since the Spirit of life is in it. It is saved through that soul. It is not forced into another flesh (body) again.

187

And I said, Lord, "Where will the souls go from those who gained knowledge but afterward turned away?" Then he said to me, "They will go to the place where the angels of misery (abject poverty) go. This is the place where there is no repentance (escape). There they will be kept with those who have blasphemed the spirit. They will be tortured and punished forever and ever. (Heb 6:4-8 and Heb 12:17-31)

I said, "Lord, from where did the false (evil) spirit come?" Then he said to me, "The Mother-Father, who is the gracious and holy of Spirit, the One who is merciful and who has compassion for all, the Thought of the Foreknowledge of light raised up the child of the perfect race and their thought was the eternal light of man."

When the head Archon realized that these people were exalted above him and their minds were stronger than him he wanted to capture their thought. He did not know that their minds were stronger and that he would not be able to capture their thoughts.

He made a plan with his agents, his powers, and they raped (committed adultery together, all of them, with) Sophia, and unbearable imprisonment (bitter fate) was born through them, which is the last unbreakable bondage. It is the kind that is unpredictable fate. This fate is harder and stronger than the gods, angels and demons and all the generations until this day together have seen. It imprisoned all through periods, seasons, and times. From that fate every sin, unrighteousness, blasphemy, forgetfulness, and ignorance and every oppressive command, and carnal sins and fear emerged. From this the whole creation was blinded, so that they may not know the God who is above them all. And because of the chain of forgetfulness, their sins were hidden from them. They are bound with measures, seasons, and time since fate is lord over everything.

When the head Archon repented for everything which had been created through him, he sought to cause a flood to destroy the works of man (Genesis 6:6). But the great light, the Foreknowledge, told Noah, and Noah announced it to all the children, the sons of men. But those who were estranged from him did not listen to him. It is not as Moses said, "They hid themselves in an ark" (Genesis 7: 7), but they hid in a certain place. Noah hid and also many other people from the immutable race. They went to a certain place and hid in a shining, glowing (enlightened) cloud. Noah understood his authority because she who is part of the light was with him.

189

She enlightened them because the head Archon darkened the entire earth.

And he planned with his agents to send his emissaries (angels) to the daughters of men so that they might take some (as wives) for themselves and raise offspring (children) for their personal enjoyment. At first they had no success so they came together again and laid a plan. They made a false spirit (like themselves), but who looked like the Spirit which had come down to them. In this way they could defile souls through it.

And the emissaries (angels) transformed themselves into the image of the husbands of the women (the daughters of men). They filled them with the spirit of darkness, which was an evil concoction they had made for them. They brought gold and silver and a gift and copper and iron and metal and all kinds of things to the angels. And they led those who followed them away into great turmoil with their lies. The people grew old without enjoying life. They died before finding truth and without knowing the God of truth. This way the entire creation was enslaved forever, from the beginning of the world until now.

And they took wives and produced children of darkness born in the image of their spirit. To this day, they closed their minds, and they hardened their hearts through the intractability of the false spirit.

I, the perfect Aeon of the All, changed myself into my own child (seed), for I existed first and have traveled every path. I am the fullness of the light. I am the remembrance of the pleroma. I sojourned to the kingdom of darkness and endured so I could I enter into the midst of this prison. The foundations of chaos shook. I disguised myself from the wicked ones, and they did not recognize me.

I returned for the second time, and I journeyed here and there. I was created from those who belong to the light, and I am that light, the perfect Aeon. I entered into the midst of darkness and depths of Hades to accomplish my task. And the foundations of chaos shook so hard they could have fallen down and killed those in chaos. I sought to root them in light so that they might not be destroyed before the time was complete.

Still for a third time I went - I am the light which exists in the light, I am the remembrance of the perfect Aeon. I entered into the midst of darkness and the depths of Hades. I filled my face with light so I could perfect (complete) their kingdom. I came into the midst of their prison, which is the prison of the body (flesh). I announced, "He who hears, let him wake up from the deep sleep." And he wept and shed tears. He wiped away bitter tears from himself and he said, "Who is it that calls my name, and from where has this hope come to me, while I am in the chains of the prison?" And I said, 'I am the perfect Aeon of the pure light; I am the thought of the pure, undefiled Spirit, who raised you up to the place of honor. Stand and remember that it is you who heard and sought your own beginnings, which is I, the merciful one. Guard yourself against the angels of bitter providence and the demons of chaos and all those who seek to entrap you Guard against the deep sleep and the cage of Hades.

And I stood him up and sealed him in the light of the water with five seals so that death might not have power over him ever again.
Now I shall go ascend to the perfect kingdom. I have told you all I have to say. And I have said everything to you that you might write it down and give them secretly to your fellow spirits. It is the mystery of the immutable race.

And the savior gave these things to John so that he might write them down and keep them intact. And he said to him, Cursed is everyone who will trade these things for a gift or for food or for water or clothing or anything. These things were presented to him in a mystery, and immediately he disappeared from him. And he went to his fellow disciples and told them what the savior had told him.

Jesus Christ, Amen.

History of The Gospel of Thomas

In the winter of 1945, in Upper Egypt, an Arab peasant was gathering fertilizer and topsoil for his crops. While digging in the soft dirt he came across a large earthen vessel. Inside were scrolls containing hitherto unseen books.

According to local lore, the boy's father had recently been killed and the lad was preparing to chase the man who had murdered his father.

The scrolls were discovered near the site of the ancient town of Chenoboskion, at the base of a mountain named Gebel et-Tarif, near Hamra-Dum, in the vicinity of Naj 'Hammadi, about sixty miles from Luxor in Egypt. The texts were written in the Coptic language and preserved on papyrus sheets. The lettering style dated them as having been penned around the third or fourth century A.D. The Gospel of Thomas is the longest of the volumes consisting of 114 verses. Recent study indicates that the original work of Thomas, of which the scrolls are copies, may predate the four canonical gospels of Matthew, Mark, Luke, and John. The origin of The Gospel of Thomas is now thought to be from the first or second century A.D.

The word Coptic is an Arabic corruption of the Greek word Aigyptos, which in turn comes from the word Hikaptah, one of the names of the city of Memphis, the first capital of ancient Egypt.

There has never been a Coptic state or government per se, however, the word has been used to generally define a culture and language present in the area of Egypt.

The known history of the Copts starts with King Mina the first King, who united the northern and southern kingdoms of Egypt circa 3050 B.C. The ancient Egyptian civilization under the rule of the Pharaohs lasted over 3000 years. Saint Mina (named after the king) is one of the major Coptic saints. He was martyred in 309 A.D.

The culture has come to be recognized as one containing distinctive art, architecture, and even a certain Christian church system.

The Coptic Church is based on the teachings of St. Mark, who introduced the region to Christianity in the first century A.D. The Copts take pride in the monastic flavor of their church and the fact that the Gospel of Mark is thought to be the oldest of the Gospels. Now, lying before a peasant boy was a scroll written in the ancient Coptic tongue: The Gospel of Thomas, possibly older than and certainly quite different from any other Gospel.

The peasant boy who found the treasure of the Gospel of Thomas stood to be rewarded greatly. This could have been the discovery of a lifetime for his family, but the boy had no idea what he had. He took the scrolls home, where his mother burned some as kindling.

Because the young man had succeeded in his pursuit of the father's murderer, he himself was now a murderer.

Fearing the authorities would soon come looking for him and not wanting to be found with ancient artifacts, he sold the codex to the black market antique dealers in Cairo for a trifle sum. It would be years until they found their way into the hands of a scholar.

Part of the thirteenth codex was smuggled from Egypt to America. In 1955 whispers of the existence of the codex had reached the ears of Gilles Quispel, a professor of religion and history in the Netherlands. The race was on to find and translate the scrolls.

The introduction of the collected sayings of Jesus refers to the writer as Didymos (Jude) Thomas. This is the same Thomas who doubted Jesus and was then told to place his hand within the breach in the side of the Savior. In the Gospel of St. John, he is referred to as Didymos, which means twin in Greek. In Aramaic, the name Jude (or Judas) also carries the sense of twin. The use of this title led some in the apocryphal tradition to believe that he was the twin brother and confidant of Jesus. However, when applied to Jesus himself, the literal meaning of twin must be rejected by orthodox Christianity as well as anyone adhering to the doctrine of the virgin birth of the only begotten Son of God. The title is likely meant to signify that Thomas was a close confidant of Jesus, or more simply, he was part of a set of twins and in no way related to Jesus.

As mentioned earlier, church historians mention that Thomas evangelized India (Asia-Minor or Central Asia).

The text has a very Eastern flavor. At times it is almost Buddhist in its wording. (For a comparative study of Zen Buddhism's Tao Te Ching and The Gospel of Thomas, see the book *The Tao Of Thomas*).

The Gospel of Thomas is actually not a gospel at all. It contains no narrative but is instead a collection of sayings, which are said to be from Jesus himself as written (quoted) by Thomas. Although the codex found in Egypt is dated to the fourth century, most biblical scholars place the actual construction of the text of Thomas at about 70 – 150 A.D. although some place it slightly later.

The gospel was often mentioned in early Christian literature, but no copy was thought to have survived until the discovery of the Coptic manuscript. Since then, part of the Oxyrynchus papyri have been identified as older Greek fragments of Thomas. The papyri were discovered in 1898 in the rubbish heaps of Oxyrhynchus, Egypt. This discovery yielded over thirty-five manuscript fragments for the New Testament. They have been dated the earliest codex found in the library to about 60 A.D. As a point of reference, a fragment of papyrus from the Dead Sea Scrolls had been dated to before 68 A.D. This is not to say that the Gospel of Thomas was dated to these years, only that the oldest books found in the library date to this time area. Thus, the collection was a very old and select one.

There are marked differences between the Greek and Coptic texts of Thomas, as we will see.

The debate on the date of Thomas centers in part on whether Thomas is dependent upon the canonical gospels, or is derived from an earlier document that was simply a collection of sayings. Many of the passages in Thomas appear to be more authentic versions of the synoptic parables, and many have parallels in Mark and Luke. This has caused a division of thought wherein some believe Thomas used common sources also used by Mark and Luke. Others believe Thomas was written independently after witnessing the same events.

If Thomas wrote his gospel first, without input from Mark, and from the standpoint of Eastern exposure as a result of his sojourn into India, it could explain the mystical quality of the text. It could also explain the striking differences in the recorded quotes of Jesus as memories were influenced by exposure to Asian culture.

There is some speculation that the sayings found in Thomas could be more accurate to the original intent and wording of Jesus than the other gospels. This may seem counter-intuitive until we realize that Christianity itself is an Eastern religion, albeit Middle-Eastern. Although as it spread west the faith went through many changes to westernize or Romanize it, Jesus was both mystical and Middle-Eastern. The Gospel of Thomas may not have seen as much "dilution" by Western society.

The Gospel of Thomas was most likely composed in Syria, where tradition holds that the church of Edessa was founded by Judas Thomas, The Twin (Didymos). The gospel may well be the earliest written tradition in the Syriac church.

The Gospel of Thomas is sometimes called a Gnostic gospel, although it seems more likely Thomas was adopted by the Gnostic community and interpreted in the light of their beliefs.

Gnostics believed that knowledge is formed or found from a personal encounter with God brought about by inward or intuitive insight. It is this knowledge that brings salvation. The Gnostics believed they were privy to a secret knowledge about the divine. It is their focus on knowledge that leads to their name.

There are numerous references to the Gnostics in second century literature. Their form of Christianity was considered heresy by the early church fathers. The intense resistance to the Gnostic belief system seems to be based in two areas. First, there was a general Gnostic belief that we were all gods, with heaven contained within us. Jesus, according to the Gnostics, was here to show us our potential to become as he was; a son or daughter of God, for God is both father and mother, male and female. These beliefs ran contrary to the newly developing orthodoxy. The second line of resistance was political. This resistance developed later and would have come from the fact that a faith based on a personal encounter flew in the face of the developing church political structure that placed priests and church as the keepers of heaven's gate with salvation through them alone.

It is from the writings condemning the group that we glean most of our information about the Gnostics. They are alluded to in the Bible in 1 Timothy 1:4 and 1 Timothy 6:20, and possibly the entirety of Jude, as the writers of the Bible defended their theology against that of the Gnostics.

The Coptic and Greek translations of The Gospel of Thomas presented herein are the result of a gestalt brought about by contrasting and comparing all of the foremost translations, where the best phrasing was chosen to follow the intent and meaning of the text.

Because there are differences between the Coptic manuscript and the Greek fragments of Thomas, each verse will have the following format for the reader to view: The Coptic text will be presented first, since we have the entire Gospel in this language. The Greek text will come next. If there is not a second rendition of the verse, the reader may assume there was no Greek fragment found for that verse or the Greek version of the verse was identical to the Coptic version. Lastly, obvious parallels found in the Bible are listed.

Let us keep in mind that some of the differences between the translations of the Greek and Coptic may be attributed in part to the choice of word or phrase of those translating. It is the differences in overall meaning of verses between Coptic and Greek on which we should focus.

In the document to follow, the Gospel of Thomas will appear as a bold text. If there are other relevant but divergent interpretations of phrases in Thomas, they are included in parentheses. Any parallels of text or meaning that appear in the Bible are placed below the verse in italicized text. Author's notes are in regular text. In this way the reader can easily identify which body of work is being referenced and observe how they fit together.

Since the deeper meanings within Thomas are both in metaphor and in plain, understandable language, it is hoped that each time the words are read some new insight and treasure can be taken from them. As we change our perspective, we see the meaning of each verse differently. As one turns a single jewel to view each facet, we should study the Gospel of Thomas in the same way.

Let us begin.

The Gospel Of Thomas

These are the secret sayings which the living Jesus has spoken and Judas who is also Thomas (the twin) (Didymos Judas Thomas) wrote. `

1. And he said: Whoever finds the interpretation of these sayings will not taste death.

1. He said to them: Whoever discovers the interpretation of these words shall never taste death.

John 8:51 Very truly I tell you, whoever keeps my word will never see death.

2. Jesus said: Let him who seeks not stop seeking until he finds, and when he finds he will be troubled, and when he has been troubled he will marvel (be astonished) and he will reign over all and in reigning, he will find rest.

2. Jesus said: Let him who seeks not stop until he finds, and when he finds he shall wonder and in wondering he shall reign, and in reigning he shall find rest.

3. Jesus said: If those who lead you say to you: Look, the Kingdom is in the sky, then the birds of the sky would enter before you. If they say to you: It is in the sea, then the fish of the sea would enter ahead of you. But the Kingdom of God exists within you and it exists outside of you. Those who come to know (recognize) themselves will find it, and when you come to know yourselves you will become known and you will realize that you are the children of the Living Father. Yet if you do not come to know yourselves then you will dwell in poverty and it will be you who are that poverty.

3. Jesus said, If those who lead you say, "See, the Kingdom is in the sky," then the birds of the sky will precede you. If they say to you, "It is under the earth," then the fish of the sea will precede you. Rather, the Kingdom of God is inside of you, and it is outside of you.

Those who come to know themselves will find it; and when you come to know yourselves, you will understand that it is you who are the sons of the living Father. But if you will not know yourselves, you dwell in poverty and it is you who are that poverty.

Luke 17:20 And when he was demanded of by the Pharisees, when the kingdom of God should come, he answered them and said, The kingdom of God cometh not with observation: Neither shall they say, Lo here! Lo there! For, behold, the kingdom of God is within you.

4. Jesus said: The person of old age will not hesitate to ask a little child of seven days about the place of life, and he will live. For many who are first will become last, (and the last will be first). And they will become one and the same.

4. Jesus said: Let the old man who has lived many days not hesitate to ask the child of seven days about the place of life; then he will live. For many that are first will be last, and last will be first, and they will become a single one.

Mark 9:35-37 He sat down, called the twelve, and said to them: Whoever wants to be first must be last of all and servant of all. Then he took a little child and put it among them, and taking it in his arms, he said to them: Whoever welcomes one such child in my name welcomes me, and whoever welcomes me welcomes not me but the one who sent me.

205

5. Jesus said: Recognize what is in front of your face, and what has been hidden from you will be revealed to you. For there is nothing hidden which will not be revealed (become manifest), and nothing buried that will not be raised.

5. Jesus said: Know what is in front of your face and what is hidden from you will be revealed to you.
For there is nothing hidden that will not be revealed.

Mark 4:2 For there is nothing hid, except to be made manifest; nor is anything secret, except it come to light.

Luke 12:3 Nothing is covered up that will not be revealed, or hidden that will not be known.

Matthew 10:26 So have no fear of them; for nothing is covered up that will not be uncovered, and nothing secret that will not become known.

6. His Disciples asked Him, they said to him: How do you want us to fast, and how will we pray? And how will we be charitable (give alms), and what laws of diet will we maintain?

Jesus said: Do not lie, and do not practice what you hate, for

everything is in the plain sight of Heaven. For there is nothing concealed that will not become manifest, and there is nothing covered that will not be exposed.

6.   His disciples asked him, "How do you want us to fast? And how shall we pray? And how shall we give alms? And what kind of diet shall we follow?"
Jesus said, don't lie, and don't do what you hate to do, for all things are revealed before the truth. For there is nothing hidden which shall not be revealed.

Luke 11:1 He was praying in a certain place, and after he had finished, one of his disciples said to him, Lord, teach us to pray, as John taught his disciples.

7. Jesus said: Blessed is the lion that the man will eat, for the lion will become the man. Cursed is the man that the lion shall eat, and still the lion will become man.

Mathew 26:20-30 He who dipped his hand with me in the dish, the same will betray me. The Son of Man goes, even as it is written of him, but woe to that man through whom the Son of Man is betrayed! It would be better for that man if he had not been born. Judas, who betrayed him, answered, "It isn't me, is it, Rabbi?" He said to him,

You said it. As they were eating, Jesus took bread, gave thanks for it, and broke it. He gave to the disciples, and said, Take, eat; this is my body. He took the cup, gave thanks, and gave to them, saying: All of you drink it, for this is my blood of the new covenant, which is poured out for many for the remission of sins. But I tell you that I will not drink of this fruit of the vine from now on, until that day when I drink it anew with you in my Father's Kingdom. When they had sung a hymn, they went out to the Mount of Olives.

8. And he said: The Kingdom of Heaven is like a wise fisherman who casts his net into the sea. He drew it up from the sea full of small fish. Among them he found a fine large fish. That wise fisherman threw all the small fish back into the sea and chose the large fish without hesitation. Whoever has ears to hear, let him hear!

Matthew 13:47-48 Again, the kingdom of heaven is like a net that was thrown into the sea and caught fish of every kind; when it was full, they drew it ashore, sat down, and put the good into baskets but threw out the bad.

9. Jesus said: Now, the sower came forth. He filled his hand and threw (the seeds). Some fell upon the road and the birds came and gathered them up. Others fell on the stone and they did not take deep enough roots in the soil, and so did not

produce grain. Others fell among the thorns and they choked the seed, and the worm ate them. Others fell upon the good earth and it produced good fruit up toward the sky, it bore 60 fold and 120 fold.

Matthew 13:3-8 And he told them many things in parables, saying: Listen! A sower went out to sow. And as he sowed, some seeds fell on the path, and the birds came and ate them up. Other seeds fell on rocky ground, where they did not have much soil, and they sprang up quickly, since they had no depth of soil. But when the sun rose, they were scorched; and since they had no root, they withered away. Other seeds fell among thorns, and the thorns grew up and choked them. Other seeds fell on good soil and brought forth grain, some a hundred fold, some sixty, some thirty.

Mark 4:2-9 And he taught them many things in parables, and in his teaching he said to them: Behold! A sower went out to sow. And as he sowed, some seed fell along the path, and the birds came and devoured it. Other seed fell on rocky ground, where it had not much soil, and immediately it sprang up, since it had no depth of soil; and when the sun rose it was scorched, and since it had no root it withered away. Other seed fell among thorns and the thorns grew up and choked it, and it yielded no grain. And other seeds fell into good soil and brought forth grain, growing up and increasing and yielding thirty fold and sixty fold and a hundred fold. And he said, He who has ears to hear, let him hear.

Luke 8:4-8 And when a great crowd came together and people from town after town came to him, he said in a parable: A sower went out to sow his seed; and as he sowed, some fell along the path, and was trodden under foot, and the birds of the air devoured it. And some fell on the rock; and as it grew up, it withered away, because it had no moisture. And some fell among thorns; and the thorns grew with it and choked it. And some fell into good soil and grew, and yielded a hundred fold. As he said this, he called out, He who has ears to hear, let him hear.

10. Jesus said: I have cast fire upon the world, and as you see, I guard it until it is ablaze.

Luke 12:49 I came to bring fire to the earth, and how I wish it were already kindled.

11. Jesus said: This sky will pass away, and the one above it will pass away. The dead are not alive, and the living will not die. In the days when you consumed what is dead, you made it alive. When you come into the Light, what will you do? On the day when you were united (one), you became separated (two). When you have become separated (two), what will you

do?

Matthew 24:35 Heaven and earth will pass away, but my words will not pass away.

12. The Disciples said to Jesus: We know that you will go away from us. Who is it that will be our teacher?

Jesus said to them: Wherever you are (in the place that you have come), you will go to James the Righteous, for whose sake Heaven and Earth were made (came into being.)

13. Jesus said to his Disciples: Compare me to others, and tell me who I am like. Simon Peter said to him: You are like a righteous messenger (angel) of God. Matthew said to him: You are like a (wise) philosopher (of the heart). Thomas said to him: Teacher, my mouth is not capable of saying who you are like!

Jesus said: I'm not your teacher, now that you have drunk; you have become drunk from the bubbling spring that I have tended (measured out). And he took him, and withdrew and spoke three words to him: ahyh ashr ahyh (I am who I am).

Now when Thomas returned to his comrades, they inquired of him: What did Jesus say to you? Thomas said to them: If I tell you even one of the words which he spoke to me, you will take up stones and throw them at me, and fire will come from the stones to consume you.

Mark 8:27-30 Jesus went on with his disciples to the villages of Caesarea Philippi; and on the way he asked his disciples, Who do people say that I am? And they answered him, John the Baptist; and others, Elijah; and still others, one of the prophets. He asked them, But who do you say that I am? Peter answered him, You are the Messiah. And he sternly ordered them not to tell anyone about him.

14. Jesus said to them: If you fast, you will give rise to transgression (sin) for yourselves. And if you pray, you will be condemned. And if you give alms, you will cause harm (evil) to your spirits. And when you go into the countryside, if they take you in (receive you) then eat what they set before you and heal the sick among them. For what goes into your mouth will not defile you, but rather what comes out of your mouth, that is what will defile you.

Luke 10:8-9 Whenever you enter a town and its people welcome you, eat what is set before you; Cure the sick who are there, and say to them, The kingdom of God has come near to you.

Mark 7:15 There is nothing outside a person that by going in can defile, but the things that come out are what defile.

Matthew 15:11 It is not what goes into the mouth that defiles a man, but what comes out of the mouth, this defiles a man.

Romans 14.14 I know and am persuaded in the Lord Jesus that nothing is unclean in itself; but it is unclean for any one who thinks it unclean.

15. Jesus said: When you see him who was not born of woman, bow yourselves down upon your faces and worship him for he is your Father.

Galatians 4:3-5 Even so we, when we were children, were in bondage under the elements of the world: But when the fullness of the time was come, God sent forth his Son, made of a woman, made under the law, To redeem them that were under the law, that we might receive the adoption of sons.

16. Jesus said: People think perhaps I have come to spread peace upon the world. They do not know that I have come to

cast dissention (conflict) upon the earth; fire, sword, war. For there will be five in a house. Three will be against two and two against three, the father against the son and the son against the father. And they will stand alone.

Matthew 10:34-36 Do not think that I have come to bring peace to the earth; I have not come to bring peace, but a sword. For I have come to set a man against his father, and a daughter against her mother, and a daughter-in-law against her mother-in-law; and one's foes will be members of one's own household.

Luke 12:51-53 Do you think that I have come to give peace on earth? No, I tell you, but rather division; for henceforth in one house there will be five divided, three against two and two against three; they will be divided, father against son and son against father, mother against daughter and daughter against her mother, mother-in-law against her daughter-in-law and daughter-in-law against her mother-in-law.

17. Jesus said: I will give to you what eye has not seen, what ear has not heard, what hand has not touched, and what has not occurred to the mind of man.

1 Cor 2:9 But, as it is written, What no eye has seen, nor ear heard, nor the human heart conceived, what God has prepared for those who love him.

18. The Disciples said to Jesus: Tell us how our end will come. Jesus said: Have you already discovered the beginning (Origin), so that you inquire about the end? Where the beginning (origin) is, there the end will be. Blessed be he who will take his place in the beginning (stand at the origin) for he will know the end, and he will not experience death.

19. Jesus said: Blessed is he who came into being before he came into being. If you become my Disciples and heed my sayings, these stones will serve you. For there are five trees in paradise for you, which are undisturbed in summer and in winter and their leaves do not fall. Whoever knows them will not experience death.

20. The Disciples said to Jesus: Tell us what the Kingdom of Heaven is like. He said to them: It is like a mustard seed, smaller than all other seeds and yet when it falls on the tilled earth, it produces a great plant and becomes shelter for the birds of the sky.

Mark 4:30-32 He also said, With what can we compare the kingdom of God, or what parable will we use for it? It is like a mustard seed, which, when sown upon the ground, is the smallest of all the seeds on earth; yet when it is sown it grows up and becomes the greatest of all shrubs, and puts forth large branches, so that the birds of the air can make nests in its shade.

Matthew 13:31-32 The kingdom of heaven is like a grain of mustard seed which a man took and sowed in his field; it is the smallest of all seeds, but when it has grown it is the greatest of shrubs and becomes a tree, so that the birds of the air come and make nests in its branches.

Luke 13.18-19 He said therefore, What is the kingdom of God like? And to what shall I compare it? It is like a grain of mustard seed which a man took and sowed in his garden; and it grew and became a tree, and the birds of the air made nests in its branches.

21. Mary said to Jesus: Who are your Disciples like? He said: They are like little children who are living in a field that is not theirs. When the owners of the field come, they will say: Let us have our field! It is as if they were naked in front of them (They undress in front of them in order to let them have what is theirs) and they give back the field. Therefore I say, if the owner of the house knows that the thief is coming, he will be alert before he arrives and will not allow him to dig

through into the house to carry away his belongings. You, must be on guard and beware of the world (system). Prepare yourself (arm yourself) with great strength or the bandits will find a way to reach you, for the problems you expect will come. Let there be among you a person of understanding (awareness). When the crop ripened, he came quickly with his sickle in his hand to reap. Whoever has ears to hear, let him hear!

Matthew 24:43 But understand this: if the owner of the house had known in what part of the night the thief was coming, he would have stayed awake and would not have let his house be broken into.

Mark 4:26-29 He also said, The kingdom of God is as if someone would scatter seed on the ground, and would sleep and rise night and day, and the seed would sprout and grow, he does not know how. The earth produces of itself, first the stalk, then the head, then the full grain in the head. But when the grain is ripe, at once he goes in with his sickle, because the harvest has come.

Luke 12:39-40 But know this, that if the householder had known at what hour the thief was coming, he would not have left his house to be broken into. You also must be ready; for the Son of man is coming at an unexpected hour.

22. Jesus saw little children who were being suckled. He said to his Disciples: These little children who are being suckled are like those who enter the Kingdom.

They said to him: Should we become like little children in order to enter the Kingdom?

Jesus said to them: When you make the two one, and you make the inside as the outside and the outside as the inside, when you make the above as the below, and if you make the male and the female one and the same (united male and female) so that the man will not be masculine (male) and the female be not feminine (female), when you establish an eye in the place of an eye and a hand in the place of a hand and a foot in the place of a foot and a likeness (image) in the place of a likeness (an image), then will you enter the Kingdom.

Luke 18:16 But Jesus called for them and said, Let the little children come to me, and do not stop them; for it is to such as these that the kingdom of God belongs. Truly I tell you, whoever does not receive the kingdom of God as a little child will never enter it.

Mark 9:43-48 If your hand causes you to stumble, cut it off; it is better for you to enter life maimed than to have two hands and to go to hell, to the unquenchable fire. And if your foot causes you to stumble, cut it off; it is better for you to enter life lame than to have two feet and to be thrown into hell. And if your eye causes you to stumble, tear it out; it is better for you to enter the kingdom of God with one eye than to have two eyes and to be thrown into hell, where the worm never dies, and the fire is never quenched.

Matthew 18:3-5 And said, Verily, I say unto you, unless you turn and become like children, you will never enter the kingdom of heaven. Whoever humbles himself like this child, he is the greatest in the kingdom of heaven. Whoever receives one such child in my name receives me;

Matthew 5:29-30 If your right eye causes you to sin, pluck it out and throw it away; it is better that you lose one of your members than that your whole body be thrown into hell. And if your right hand causes you to sin, cut it off and throw it away; it is better that you lose one of your members than that your whole body go into hell.

23. Jesus said: I will choose you, one out of a thousand and two out of ten thousand and they will stand as a single one.

Matthew 20:16 So the last shall be first, and the first last: for many be called, but few chosen.

24. His Disciples said: Show us the place where you are (your place), for it is necessary for us to seek it.

24. He said to them: Whoever has ears, let him hear! Within a man of light there is light, and he illumines the entire world. If he does not shine, he is darkness (there is darkness).

John13:36 Simon Peter said to him, Lord, where are you going? Jesus answered, Where I am going, you cannot follow me now; but you will follow afterward.

Matthew 6:22-23 The eye is the lamp of the body. So, if your eye is healthy, your whole body will be full of light; but if your eye is unhealthy, your whole body will be full of darkness. If then the light in you is darkness, how great is the darkness!

Luke 11:34-36 Your eye is the lamp of your body; when your eye is sound, your whole body is full of light; but when it is not sound, your body is full of darkness. Therefore be careful lest the light in you be darkness. If then your whole body is full of light, having no part dark, it will be wholly bright, as when a lamp with its rays gives you light.

Author's Note:

Early philosophers thought that light was transmitted from the eye and bounced back, allowing the person to sense the world at large. Ancient myths tell of Aphrodite constructing the human eye out of the four elements (earth, wind, fire, and water). The eye was held together by love. She kindled the fire of the soul and used it to project from the eyes so that it would act like a lantern, transmitting the light, thus allowing us to see.

Euclid, (330 BC to 260BC) speculated about the speed of light being instantaneous since you close your eyes, then open them again; even the distant objects appear immediately.

25. Jesus said: Love your friend (Brother) as your soul; protect him as you would the pupil of your own eye.

Romans 12:9-11 Let love be without dissimulation. Abhor that which is evil; cleave to that which is good. Be kindly affectioned one to another with brotherly love; in honour preferring one another; Not slothful in business; fervent in spirit; serving the Lord...

26. Jesus said: You see the speck in your brother's eye but the beam that is in your own eye you do not see. When you remove the beam out of your own eye, then will you see

clearly to remove the speck out of your brother's eye.

26.   Jesus said, You see the splinter in your brother's eye, but you don't see the log in your own eye. When you take the log out of your own eye, then you will see well enough to remove the splinter from your brother's eye.

Matthew 7:3-5 Why do you see the speck in your neighbor's eye, but do not notice the log in your own eye? Or how can you say to your neighbor, Let me take the speck out of your eye, while the log is in your own eye? You hypocrite, first take the log out of your own eye, and then you will see clearly to take the speck out of your neighbor's eye.

Luke 6:41-42 Why do you see the speck that is in your brother's eye, but do not notice the log that is in your own eye? Or how can you say to your brother, Brother, let me take out the speck that is in your eye, when you yourself do not see the log that is in your own eye? You hypocrite, first take the log out of your own eye, and then you will see clearly to take out the speck that is in your brother's eye.

27. Jesus said: Unless you fast from the world (system), you will not find the Kingdom of God. Unless you keep the Sabbath (entire week) as Sabbath, you will not see the Father.

27. Jesus said: Unless you fast (abstain) from the world, you shall in no way find the Kingdom of God; and unless you observe the Sabbath as a Sabbath, you shall not see the Father.

28. Jesus said: I stood in the midst of the world. In the flesh I appeared to them. I found them all drunk; I found none thirsty among them. My soul grieved for the sons of men, for they are blind in their hearts and do not see that they came into the world empty, they are destined (determined) to leave the world empty. However, now they are drunk. When they have shaken off their wine, then they will repent (change their ways).

28. Jesus said: I took my stand in the midst of the world, and they saw me in the flesh, and I found they were all drunk, and I found none of them were thirsty. And my soul grieved over the souls of men because they are blind in their hearts. They do not see that they came into the world empty, therefore they are determined to leave the world empty. However, now they are drunk. When they have shaken off their wine, then they will change their ways.

29. Jesus said: If the flesh came into being because of spirit, it is a marvel, but if spirit came into being because of the body, it would be a marvel of marvels. I marvel indeed at how great wealth has taken up residence in this poverty.

30. Jesus said: Where there are three gods, they are gods (Where there are three gods they are without god). Where there is only one, I say that I am with him. Lift the stone and there you will find me, Split the wood and there am I.

30. Jesus said: Where three are together they are not without God, and when there is one alone, I say, I am with him.

Author's Note:
Many scholars believe pages of the manuscript were misplaced and verses 30 and 77 should run together as a single verse.

77. Jesus said: I-Am the Light who is over all things, I-Am the All. From me all came forth and to me all return (The All came from me and the All has come to me). Split wood, there am I. Lift up the stone and there you will find me.

Matthew 18:20 For where two or three are gathered in my name, I am there among them.

31. Jesus said: No prophet is accepted in his own village, no physician heals those who know him.

31. Jesus said: A prophet is not accepted in his own country, neither can a doctor cure those that know him.

Mark 6:4 Then Jesus said to them, Prophets are not without honor, except in their hometown, and among their own kin, and in their own house.

Matthew 13:57 And they took offense at him. But Jesus said to them: A prophet is not without honor save in his own country and in his own house.

Luke 4:24 And he said, Truly, I say to you, no prophet is acceptable in his own country.

John 4:43-44 After the two days he departed to Galilee. For Jesus himself testified that a prophet has no honor in his own country.

32. Jesus said: A city being built (and established) upon a high mountain and fortified cannot fall nor can it be hidden.

32. Jesus said: A city built on a high hilltop and fortified can neither fall nor be hidden.

Matthew 5:14 You are the light of the world. A city built on a hill cannot be hid.

33. Jesus said: What you will hear in your ear preach from your rooftops. For no one lights a lamp and sets it under a basket nor puts it in a hidden place, but rather it is placed on a lamp stand so that everyone who comes and goes will see its light.

33. Jesus said: What you hear with one ear preach from your rooftops. For no one lights a lamp and sets it under a basket or hides, but rather it is placed on a lamp stand so that everyone who comes and goes will see its light.

Matthew 10:27 What I say to you in the dark, tell in the light; and what you hear whispered, proclaim from the housetops.

Luke 8:16 No one after lighting a lamp hides it under a jar, or puts it under a bed, but puts it on a lamp stand, so that those who enter may see the light.

Matthew 5:15 Nor do men light a lamp and put it under a bushel, but on a stand, and it gives light to all in the house.

Mark 4:21 And he said to them, Is a lamp brought in to be put under a bushel, or under a bed, and not on a stand?

Luke 11:33 No one after lighting a lamp puts it in a cellar or under a bushel, but on a stand, that those who enter may see the light.

34. Jesus said: If a blind person leads a blind person, both fall into a pit.

Matthew 15:14 Let them alone; they are blind guides of the blind. And if one blind person guides another, both will fall into a pit.

Luke 6:39 He also told them a parable: Can a blind man lead a blind man? Will they not both fall into a pit?

35. Jesus said: It is impossible for anyone to enter the house of a strong man to take it by force unless he binds his hands, then he will be able to loot his house.

Matthew 12:29 Or how can one enter a strong man's house and plunder his goods, unless he first binds the strong man? Then indeed he may plunder his house.

Luke 11:21-22 When a strong man, fully armed, guards his own palace, his goods are in peace; but when one stronger than he assails him and overcomes him, he takes away his armor in which he trusted, and divides his spoil.

Mark 3:27 But no one can enter a strong man's house and plunder his property without first tying up the strong man; then indeed the house can be plundered.

36. Jesus said: Do not worry from morning to evening nor from evening to morning about the food that you will eat nor about what clothes you will wear. You are much superior to the Lilies which neither card nor spin. When you have no clothing, what do you wear? Who can add time to your life (increase your stature)? He himself will give to you your garment.

Matthew 6:25-31 Therefore I tell you, do not worry about your life, what you will eat or what you will drink, or about your body, what you will wear. Is not life more than food, and the body more than clothing? Look at the birds of the air; they neither sow nor reap nor gather into barns, and yet your heavenly Father feeds them. Are you not of more value than they? And can any of you by worrying add a single hour to your span of life? And why do you worry about clothing? Consider the lilies of the field, how they grow; they neither toil nor spin, yet I tell you, even Solomon in all his glory was not clothed like one of these. But if God so clothes the grass of the field, which is alive today and tomorrow is thrown into the oven, will he not much more clothe you--you of little faith? Therefore do not worry, saying, What will we eat? or What will we drink? or What will we wear?

Luke 12:22-23 And he said to his disciples, Therefore I tell you, do not be anxious about your life, what you shall eat, nor about your body, what you shall put on. For life is more than food, and the body more than clothing.

37. His Disciples said: When will you appear to us, and when will we see you?

Jesus said: When you take off your garments without being ashamed, and place your garments under your feet and tread on them as the little children do, then will you see the Son of the Living-One, and you will not be afraid.

37 His disciples said to him, when will you be visible to us, and when shall we be able to see you?

He said, when you strip naked without being ashamed and place your garments under your feet and tread on them as the

little children do, then will you see the Son of the Living-One, and you will not be afraid.

38. Jesus said: Many times have you yearned to hear these sayings which I speak to you, and you have no one else from whom to hear them. There will be days when you will seek me but you will not find me.

39. Jesus said: The Pharisees and the Scribes have received the keys of knowledge, but they have hidden them. They did not go in, nor did they permit those who wished to enter to do so. However, you be as wise (astute) as serpents and innocent as doves.

39. Jesus said: The Pharisees and the Scribes have stolen the keys of heaven, but they have hidden them. They have entered in, but they did not permit those who wished to enter to do so. However, you be as wise as serpents and innocent as doves.

Luke 11:52 Woe to you lawyers! For you have taken away the key of knowledge; you did not enter yourselves, and you hindered those who were entering.

Matthew 10:16 See, I am sending you out like sheep into the midst of wolves; so be wise as serpents and innocent as doves.

Matthew 23.13 But woe unto you, scribes and Pharisees, hypocrites! because you shut the kingdom of heaven against men; for you neither enter yourselves, nor allow those who would enter to go in.

40. Jesus said: A grapevine has been planted outside the (vineyard of the) Father, and since it is not viable (supported) it will be pulled up by its roots and destroyed.

Matthew 15:13 He answered, Every plant that my heavenly Father has not planted will be uprooted.

41. Jesus said: Whoever has (it) in his hand, to him will (more) be given. And whoever does not have, from him will be taken even the small amount which he has.

Matthew 25:29 For to all those who have, more will be given, and they will have an abundance; but from those who have nothing, even what they have will be taken away.

Luke 19:26 I tell you, that to every one who has will more be given; but from him who has not, even what he has will be taken away.

42. Jesus said: Become passers-by.

43. His Disciples said to him: Who are you, that you said these things to us?

Jesus said to them: You do not recognize who I am from what I said to you, but rather you have become like the Jews who either love the tree and hate its fruit, or love the fruit and hate the tree.

John 8:25 They said to him, Who are you? Jesus said to them, Why do I speak to you at all?

Matthew 7:16-20 You will know them by their fruits. Are grapes gathered from thorns, or figs from thistles? In the same way, every good tree bears good fruit, but the bad tree bears bad fruit. A good tree cannot bear bad fruit, nor can a bad tree bear good fruit. Every tree that does not bear good fruit is cut down and thrown into the fire. Thus you will know them by their fruits.

44. Jesus said: Whoever blasphemes against the Father, it will be forgiven him. And whoever blasphemes against the Son, it will be forgiven him. Yet whoever blasphemes against the Holy Spirit, it will not be forgiven him neither on earth nor in heaven.

Mark 3:28-29 Truly I tell you, people will be forgiven for their sins and whatever blasphemies they utter; but whoever blasphemes against the Holy Spirit can never have forgiveness, but is guilty of an eternal sin.

Matthew 12:31-32 Therefore I tell you, every sin and blasphemy will be forgiven men, but the blasphemy against the Spirit will not be forgiven. And whoever says a word against the Son of man will be forgiven; but whoever speaks against the Holy Spirit will not be forgiven, either in this age or in the age to come.

Luke 12:10 And every one who speaks a word against the Son of man will be forgiven him; but he who blasphemes against the Holy Spirit will not be forgiven.

45. Jesus said: Grapes are not harvested from thorns, nor are figs gathered from thistles, for they do not give fruit. A good person brings forth goodness out of his storehouse. A bad person brings forth evil out of his evil storehouse which is in his heart, and he speaks evil, for out of the abundance of the heart he brings forth evil.

Luke 6:43-45 For no good tree bears bad fruit, nor again does a bad tree bear good fruit; for each tree is known by its own fruit. For figs are not gathered from thorns, nor are grapes picked from a bramble

233

bush. The good man out of the good treasure of his heart produces good, and the evil man out of his evil treasure produces evil; for out of the abundance of the heart his mouth speaks.

46. Jesus said: From Adam until John the Baptist there is none born of women who surpasses John the Baptist, so that his eyes should not be downcast (lowered). Yet I have said that whoever among you becomes like a child will know the Kingdom, and he will be greater than John.

Matthew 11:11 Truly I tell you, among those born of women no one has arisen greater than John the Baptist; yet the least in the kingdom of heaven is greater than he.

Luke 7:28 I tell you, among those born of women none is greater than John; yet he who is least in the kingdom of God is greater than he.

Matthew 18:2-4 He called a child, whom he put among them, and said, Truly I tell you, unless you change and become like children, you will never enter the kingdom of heaven. Whoever becomes humble like this child is the greatest in the kingdom of heaven.

47. Jesus said: It is impossible for a man to mount two horses or to draw two bows, and a servant cannot serve two masters, otherwise he will honor the one and disrespect the other. No

man drinks vintage wine and immediately desires to drink new wine, and they do not put new wine into old wineskins or they would burst, and they do not put vintage wine into new wineskins or it would spoil (sour). They do not sew an old patch on a new garment because that would cause a split.

Matthew 6:24 No one can serve two masters; for a slave will either hate the one and love the other, or be devoted to the one and despise the other. You cannot serve God and wealth.

Matthew 9:16-17 No one sews a piece of cloth, not yet shrunk, on an old cloak, for the patch pulls away from the cloak, and a worse tear is made. Neither is new wine put into old wineskins; otherwise, the skins burst, and the wine is spilled, and the skins are destroyed; but new wine is put into fresh wineskins, and so both are preserved.

Mark 2:21-22 No one sews a piece of unshrunk cloth on an old garment; if he does, the patch tears away from it, the new from the old, and a worse tear is made. And no one puts new wine into old wineskins; if he does, the wine will burst the skins, and the wine is lost, and so are the skins; but new wine is for fresh skins.

Luke 5:36-39 He told them a parable also: No one tears a piece from a new garment and puts it upon an old garment; if he does, he will tear the new, and the piece from the new will not match the old. And no one puts new wine into old wineskins; if he does, the new wine will burst the skins and it will be spilled, and the skins will be destroyed. But new wine must be put into fresh wineskins. And no one after drinking old wine desires new; for he says, "The old is good."

48. Jesus said: If two make peace with each other in this one house, they will say to the mountain: Be moved! and it will be moved.

Matthew 18:19 Again, truly I tell you, if two of you agree on earth about anything you ask, it will be done for you by my Father in heaven.

Mark 11:23-24 Truly I tell you, if you say to this mountain, Be taken up and thrown into the sea, and if you do not doubt in your heart, but believe that what you say will come to pass, it will be done for you. So I tell you, whatever you ask for in prayer, believe that you have received it, and it will be yours.

Matthew 17:20 He said to them, Because of your little faith. For truly, I say to you, if you have faith as a grain of mustard seed, you will say to this mountain, Move from here to there, and it will move; and nothing will be impossible to you.

49. Jesus said: Blessed is the solitary and chosen, for you will find the Kingdom. You have come from it, and unto it you

will return.

Matthew 5:1-3 And seeing the multitudes, he went up into a mountain: and when he was set, his disciples came unto him: And he opened his mouth, and taught them, saying, Blessed are the poor in spirit: for theirs is the kingdom of heaven.

John 20:28-30 And Thomas answered and said unto him, My LORD and my God. Jesus saith unto him, Thomas, because thou hast seen me, thou hast believed: blessed are they that have not seen, and yet have believed. And many other signs truly did Jesus in the presence of his disciples, which are not written in this book:

50. Jesus said: If they say to you: From where do you come? Say to them: We have come from the Light, the place where the Light came into existence of its own accord and he stood and appeared in their image. If they say to you: Is it you? (Who are you?), say: We are his Sons and we are the chosen of the Living Father. If they ask you: What is the sign of your Father in you? Say to them: It is movement with rest (peace in the midst of motion or chaos).

51. His Disciples said to him: When will the rest of the dead occur, and when will the New World come? He said to them: That which you look for has already come, but you do not

recognize it.

52. His Disciples said to him: Twenty-four prophets preached in Israel, and they all spoke of you (in your spirit). He said to them: You have ignored the Living-One who is in your presence and you have spoken only of the dead.

53. His Disciples said to him: Is circumcision beneficial or not? He said to them: If it were beneficial, their father would beget them already circumcised from their mother. However, the true spiritual circumcision has become entirely beneficial.

Jeremiah 4:3-5 For thus saith the LORD to the men of Judah and Jerusalem, Break up your fallow ground, and sow not among thorns. Circumcise yourselves to the LORD, and take away the foreskins of your heart, ye men of Judah and inhabitants of Jerusalem: lest my fury come forth like fire, and burn that none can quench it, because of the evil of your doings. Declare ye in Judah, and publish in Jerusalem; and say, Blow ye the trumpet in the land: cry, gather together, and say, Assemble yourselves, and let us go into the defenced cities.

54. Jesus said: Blessed be the poor, for yours is the Kingdom of the Heaven.

Matthew 6:20 Then he looked up at his disciples and said: Blessed are you who are poor, for yours is the kingdom of God.

Luke 6:20 And he lifted up his eyes on his disciples, and said: Blessed are you poor, for yours is the kingdom of God.

Matthew 5:3 Blessed are the poor in spirit, for theirs is the kingdom of heaven.

55. Jesus said: Whoever does not hate his father and his mother will not be able to become my Disciple. And whoever does not hate his brothers and his sisters and does not take up his own cross in my way, will not become worthy of me.

Luke 14:26-27 If any one comes to me and does not hate his own father and mother and wife and children and brothers and sisters, yes, and even his own life, he cannot be my disciple. Whoever does not bear his own cross and come after me, cannot be my disciple.

John 17:11-21 And now I am no more in the world, but these are in the world, and I come to thee. Holy Father, keep through thine own name those whom thou hast given me, that they may be one, as we are. While I was with them in the world, I kept them in thy name: those that thou gavest me I have kept, and none of them is lost, but the son of perdition; that the scripture might be fulfilled. And now come I to thee; and these things I speak in the world, that they might have my joy fulfilled in themselves. I have given them thy word; and the world hath hated them, because they are not of the world, even as I am not of the world. I pray not that thou shouldest take them out of the world, but that thou shouldest keep them from the evil. They are not of the world, even as I am not of the world. Sanctify them through thy truth: thy word is truth. As thou hast sent me into the world, even so have I also sent them into the world. And for their sakes I sanctify myself, that they also might be sanctified through the truth. Neither pray I for these alone, but for them also which shall believe on me through their word; That they all may be one; as thou, Father, art in me, and I in thee, that they also may be one in us: that the world may believe that thou hast sent me.

56. Jesus said: Whoever has come to understand the world (system) has found a corpse, and whoever has found a corpse, is superior to the world (of him the system is not worthy).

Hebrews 11:37-40 They were stoned, they were sawn asunder, were tempted, were slain with the sword: they wandered about in sheepskins and goatskins; being destitute, afflicted, tormented; (Of whom the world was not worthy:) they wandered in deserts, and in mountains, and in dens and caves of the earth. And these all, having obtained a good report through faith, received not the promise: God having provided some better thing for us, that they without us should not be made perfect.

57. Jesus said: The Kingdom of the Father is like a person who has good seed. His enemy came by night and sowed a weed among the good seed. The man did not permit them to pull up the weed, he said to them: perhaps you will intend to pull up the weed and you pull up the wheat along with it. But, on the day of harvest the weeds will be very visible and then they will pull them and burn them.

Matthew 13:24-30 He put before them another parable: The kingdom of heaven may be compared to someone who sowed good seed in his field; but while everybody was asleep, an enemy came and sowed weeds among the wheat, and then went away. So when the plants came up and bore grain, then the weeds appeared as well. And the slaves of the householder came and said to him, Master, did you not sow good seed in your field? Where, then, did these weeds come from? He answered, An enemy has done this. The slaves said to him, Then do you want us to go and gather them? But he replied, No; for in gathering the weeds you would uproot the wheat along with them. Let both of them grow together until the harvest; and at harvest time I will tell the reapers, Collect the weeds first and bind them in bundles to be burned, but gather the wheat into my barn.

58. Jesus said: Blessed is the person who has suffered, for he

has found life. (Blessed is he who has suffered to find life and found life).

Matthew 11:28 Come to me, all you that are weary and are carrying heavy burdens, and I will give you rest.

59. Jesus said: Look to the Living-One while you are alive, otherwise, you might die and seek to see him and will be unable to find him.

John 7:34 You will search for me, but you will not find me; and where I am, you cannot come.

John 13:33 Little children, I am with you only a little longer. You will look for me; and as I said to the Jews so now I say to you, Where I am going, you cannot come.

60. They saw a Samaritan carrying a lamb, on his way to Judea. Jesus said to them: Why does he take the lamb with him? They said to him: So that he may kill it and eat it. He said to them: While it is alive he will not eat it, but only after he kills it and it becomes a corpse. They said: How could he do otherwise? He said to them: Look for a place of rest for yourselves, otherwise, you might become corpses and be eaten.

61. Jesus said: Two will rest on a bed and one will die and the other will live. Salome said: Who are you, man? As if sent by someone, you laid upon my bed and you ate from my table. Jesus said to her: I-Am he who is from that which is whole (the undivided). I have been given the things of my Father. Salome said: I'm your Disciple. Jesus said to her: Thus, I say that whenever someone is one (undivided)
he will be filled with light, yet whenever he is divided (chooses) he will be filled with darkness.

Luke 17:34 I tell you, on that night there will be two in one bed; one will be taken and the other left.

62. Jesus said: I tell my mysteries to those who are worthy of my mysteries. Do not let your right hand know what your left hand is doing.

Mark 4:11 And he said to them, To you has been given the secret of the kingdom of God, but for those outside, everything comes in parables.

Matthew 6:3 But when you give alms, do not let your left hand know what your right hand is doing.

Luke 8:10 He said, To you it has been given to know the secrets of the kingdom of God; but for others they are in parables, so that seeing they may not see, and hearing they may not understand.

Matthew 13:10-11 Then the disciples came and said to him, Why do you speak to them in parables? And he answered them, To you it has been given to know the secrets of the kingdom of heaven, but to them it has not been given.

63. Jesus said: There was a wealthy person who had much money, and he said: I will use my money so that I may sow and reap and replant, to fill my storehouses with grain so that I lack nothing. This was his intention (is what he thought in his heart) but that same night he died. Whoever has ears, let him hear!

Luke 12:21 Then he told them a parable: The land of a rich man produced abundantly. And he thought to himself, What should I do, for I have no place to store my crops? Then he said, I will do this: I will pull down my barns and build larger ones, and there I will store all my grain and my goods. And I will say to my soul, Soul, you have ample goods laid up for many years; relax, eat, drink, be merry. But God said to him, You fool! This very night your life is being demanded of you. And the things you have prepared, whose will they be? So it is with those who store up treasures for themselves but are not rich toward God.

64. Jesus said: A person had houseguests, and when he had prepared the banquet in their honor he sent his servant to invite the guests. He went to the first, he said to him: My master invites you. He replied: I have to do business with some merchants. They are coming to see me this evening. I will go to place my orders with them. I ask to be excused from the banquet. He went to another, he said to him: My master has invited you. He replied to him: I have just bought a house and they require me for a day. I will have no spare time. He came to another, he said to him: My master invites you. He replied to him: My friend is getting married and I must arrange a banquet for him. I will not be able to come. I ask to be excused from the banquet. He went to another, he said to him: My master invites you. He replied to him: I have bought a farm. I go to receive the rent. I will not be able to come. I ask to be excused. The servant returned, he said to his master: Those whom you have invited to the banquet have excused themselves. The master said to his servant: Go out to the roads, bring those whom you find so that they may feast. And he said: Businessmen and merchants will not enter the places of my Father.

Luke 14:16-24 Then Jesus said to him:, Someone gave a great dinner and invited many. At the time for the dinner he sent his slave to say to those who had been invited, Come; for everything is ready now. But they all alike began to make excuses. The first said to him, I have bought a piece of land, and I must go out and see it; please accept my regrets. Another said, I have bought five yoke of oxen, and I am going to try them out; please accept my regrets. Another said, I have just been married, and therefore I cannot come. So the slave returned and reported this to his master. Then the owner of the house became angry and said to his slave, Go out at once into the streets and lanes of the town and bring in the poor, the crippled, the blind, and the lame. And the slave said, Sir, what you ordered has been done, and there is still room. Then the master said to the slave, Go out into the roads and lanes, and compel people to come in, so that my house may be filled. For I tell you, none of those who were invited will taste my dinner.

Matthew 19:23 Then Jesus said to his disciples, Truly I tell you, it will be hard for a rich person to enter the kingdom of heaven.

Matthew 22:1-14 And Jesus answered and spake unto them again by parables, and said, The kingdom of heaven is like unto a certain king, which made a marriage for his son, and sent his servants to call those who were invited to the marriage feast; but they would not come. Again he sent other servants, saying, Tell those who are invited, Behold, I have made ready my dinner, my oxen and my fat calves are killed, and everything is ready; come to the marriage feast. But they made light of it and went off, one to his farm, another to his business, while the rest seized his servants, treated them shamefully, and killed them. The king was angry, and he sent his troops and destroyed those murderers and burned their city. Then he said to his servants, The wedding is ready, but those invited were not worthy. Go therefore to the thoroughfares, and invite to the marriage feast as many as you find. And those servants went out into the streets and gathered all whom they found, both bad and good; so the wedding hall was filled with guests. But when the king came in to look at the guests, he saw there a man who had no wedding garment; and he said to him, Friend, how did you get in here without a wedding garment? And he was speechless. Then the king said to the attendants, Bind him hand and foot, and cast him into the outer darkness; there men will weep and gnash their teeth. For many are called, but few are chosen.

65. He said: A kind person who owned a vineyard leased it to tenants so that they would work it and he would receive the fruit from them. He sent his servant so that the tenants would give to him the fruit of the vineyard. They seized his servant and beat him nearly to death. The servant went, he told his master what had happened. His master said: Perhaps they did not recognize him. So, he sent another servant. The tenants beat him also. Then the owner sent his son. He said:

Perhaps they will respect my son. Since the tenants knew that he was the heir to the vineyard, they seized him and killed him. Whoever has ears, let him hear!

Matthew 21:33-39 Listen to another parable. There was a landowner who planted a vineyard, put a fence around it, dug a wine press in it, and built a watchtower. Then he leased it to tenants and went to another country. When the harvest time had come, he sent his slaves to the tenants to collect his produce. But the tenants seized his slaves and beat one, killed another, and stoned another. Again he sent other slaves, more than the first; and they treated them in the same way. Finally he sent his son to them, saying, They will respect my son. But when the tenants saw the son, they said to themselves, This is the heir; come, let us kill him and get his inheritance. So they seized him, threw him out of the vineyard, and killed him.

Mark 12:1-9 And he began to speak to them in parables. A man planted a vineyard, and set a hedge around it, and dug a pit for the wine press, and built a tower, and let it out to tenants, and went into another country. When the time came, he sent a servant to the tenants, to get from them some of the fruit of the vineyard. And they took him and beat him, and sent him away empty-handed. Again he sent to them another servant, and they wounded him in the head, and treated him shamefully. And he sent another, and him they killed; and so with many others, some they beat and some they killed. He had still one other, a beloved son; finally he sent him to them, saying, They will respect my son. But those tenants said to one another, This is the heir; come, let us kill him, and the inheritance will be ours. And they took him and killed him, and cast him out of the vineyard. What will the owner of the vineyard do? He will come and destroy the tenants, and give the vineyard to others.

Luke 20:9-16 And he began to tell the people this parable: A man planted a vineyard, and let it out to tenants, and went into another country for a long while. When the time came, he sent a servant to the tenants, that they should give him some of the fruit of the vineyard; but the tenants beat him, and sent him away empty-handed. And he sent another servant; him also they beat and treated shamefully, and sent him away empty-handed. And he sent yet a third; this one they wounded and cast out. Then the owner of the vineyard said, What shall I do? I will send my beloved son; it may be they will respect him. But when the tenants saw him, they said to themselves, This is the heir; let us kill him, that the inheritance may be ours. And they cast him out of the vineyard and killed him. What then will the owner of the vineyard do to them? He will come and destroy those tenants, and give the vineyard to others. When they heard this, they said, God forbid!

66. Jesus said: Show me the stone which the builders have rejected. It is that one that is the cornerstone (keystone).

Matthew 21:42 Jesus said to them, Have you never read in the scriptures: The very stone which the builders rejected has become the head of the corner; this was the Lord's doing, and it is marvelous in our eyes?

Mark 12:10-11 Have you not read this scripture: The very stone which the builders rejected has become the head of the corner; this was the Lord's doing, and it is marvelous in our eyes?

Luke 20:17 But he looked at them and said, What then does this text mean: The stone that the builders rejected has become the cornerstone?

67. Jesus said: Those who know everything but themselves, lack everything. (whoever knows the all and still feels a personal lacking, he is completely deficient).

Jeremiah 17:5- 10 Thus saith the LORD; Cursed be the man that trusteth in man, and maketh flesh his arm, and whose heart departeth from the LORD. For he shall be like the heath in the desert, and shall not see when good cometh; but shall inhabit the parched places in the wilderness, in a salt land and not inhabited. Blessed is the man that trusteth in the LORD, and whose hope the LORD is. For he shall be as a tree planted by the waters, and that spreadeth out her roots by the river, and shall not see when heat cometh, but her leaf shall be green; and shall not be careful in the year of drought, neither shall cease from yielding fruit. The heart is deceitful above all things, and desperately wicked: who can know it? I the LORD search the heart, I try the reins, even to give every man according to his ways, and according to the fruit of his doings.

68. Jesus said: Blessed are you when you are hated and persecuted, but they themselves will find no reason why you have been persecuted.

Matthew 5:11 Blessed are you when people revile you and persecute you and utter all kinds of evil against you falsely on my account.

Luke 6:22 Blessed are you when men hate you, and when they exclude you and revile you, and cast out your name as evil, on account of the Son of man!

69. Jesus said: Blessed are those who have been persecuted in their heart; these are they who have come to know the Father in truth. Jesus said: Blessed are the hungry, for the stomach of him who desires to be filled will be filled.

Matthew 5:8 Blessed are the pure in heart, for they will see God.

Luke 6:21 Blessed are you who are hungry now, for you will be filled.

70. Jesus said: If you bring forth what is within you, it will save you. If you do not have it within you to bring forth, that which you lack will destroy you.

71. Jesus said: I will destroy this house, and no one will be able to build it again.

Mark 14:58 We heard him say, I will destroy this temple that is made with hands, and in three days I will build another, not made with hands.

72. A person said to him: Tell my brothers to divide the possessions of my father with me. He said to him: Oh man, who made me a divider? He turned to his Disciples, he said to them: I'm not a divider, am I?

Luke 12:13-15 Someone in the crowd said to him, Teacher, tell my brother to divide the family inheritance with me. But he said to him, Friend, who set me to be a judge or arbitrator over you? And he said to them, Take care! Be on your guard against all kinds of greed; for one's life does not consist in the abundance of possessions.

73.   Jesus said: The harvest is indeed plentiful, but the workers are few. Ask the Lord to send workers for the harvest.

Matthew 9:37-38 Then he said to his disciples, The harvest is plentiful, but the laborers are few; therefore ask the Lord of the harvest to send out laborers into his harvest.

74. He said: Lord, there are many around the well, yet there is nothing in the well. How is it that many are around the well and no one goes into it?

75. Jesus said: There are many standing at the door, but only those who are alone are the ones who will enter into the Bridal Chamber.

Matthew 25:1-8 Then shall the kingdom of heaven be likened unto ten virgins, which took their lamps, and went forth to meet the bridegroom. And five of them were wise, and five were foolish. They that were foolish took their lamps, and took no oil with them: But the wise took oil in their vessels with their lamps. While the bridegroom tarried, they all slumbered and slept. And at midnight there was a cry made, Behold, the bridegroom cometh; go ye out to meet him. Then all those virgins arose, and trimmed their lamps. And the foolish said unto the wise, Give us of your oil; for our lamps are gone out.

76. Jesus said: The Kingdom of the Father is like a rich merchant who found a pearl. The merchant was prudent. He sold his fortune and bought the one pearl for himself. You also, seek for his treasure which does not fail, which endures where no moth can come near to eat it nor worm to devour it.

Matthew 13:45-46 Again, the kingdom of heaven is like a merchant in search of fine pearls; on finding one pearl of great value, he went and sold all that he had and bought it.

Matthew 6:19-20 Do not store up for yourselves treasures on earth, where moth and rust consume and where thieves break in and steal; but store up for yourselves treasures in heaven, where neither moth nor rust consumes and where thieves do not break in and steal.

77. Jesus said: I-Am the Light who is over all things, I-Am the All. From me all came forth and to me all return (The All came from me and the All has come to me). Split wood, there am I. Lift up the stone and there you will find me.

Author's Note:
Many scholars believe the order of verses 30 and 77 were misplaced and these two verses should be connected as one verse.

30. Jesus said: Where there are three gods, they are gods (Where there are three gods they are without god). Where there is only one, I say that I am with him. Lift the stone and there you will find me, Split the wood and there am I.

John 8:12 Again Jesus spoke to them, saying, I am the light of the world. Whoever follows me will never walk in darkness but will have the light of life.

John 1:3 All things came into being through him, and without him not one thing came into being.

78. Jesus said: Why did you come out to the wilderness; to see a reed shaken by the wind? And to see a person dressed in fine (soft – plush) garments like your rulers and your dignitaries? They are clothed in plush garments, and they are not able to recognize (understand) the truth.

Matthew 11:7-9 As they went away, Jesus began to speak to the crowds about John: What did you go out into the wilderness to look at? A reed shaken by the wind? What then did you go out to see? Someone dressed in soft robes? Look, those who wear soft robes are in royal palaces. What then did you go out to see? A prophet? Yes, I tell you, and more than a prophet.

79. A woman from the multitude said to him: Blessed is the womb which bore you, and the breasts which nursed you! He said to her: Blessed are those who have heard the word (meaning) of the Father and have truly kept it. For there will be days when you will say: Blessed be the womb which has

not conceived and the breasts which have not nursed.

Luke 11:27-28 While he was saying this, a woman in the crowd raised her voice and said to him, Blessed is the womb that bore you and the breasts that nursed you! But he said, Blessed rather are those who hear the word of God and obey it!

Luke 23:29 For the days are surely coming when they will say, Blessed are the barren, and the wombs that never bore, and the breasts that never nursed.

80. Jesus said: Whoever has come to understand (recognize) the world (world system) has found the body (corpse), and whoever has found the body (corpse), of him the world (world system) is not worthy.

Hebrews 11:37-40 They were stoned, they were sawn asunder, were tempted, were slain with the sword: they wandered about in sheepskins and goatskins; being destitute, afflicted, tormented; (Of whom the world was not worthy:) they wandered in deserts, and in mountains, and in dens and caves of the earth. And these all, having obtained a good report through faith, received not the promise: God having provided some better thing for us, that they without us should not be made perfect.

81. Jesus said: Whoever has become rich should reign, and let whoever has power renounce it.

82. Jesus said: Whoever is close to me is close to the fire, and whoever is far from me is far from the Kingdom.

John 14:6-9 Jesus saith unto him, I am the way, the truth, and the life: no man cometh unto the Father, but by me. If ye had known me, ye should have known my Father also: and from henceforth ye know him, and have seen him. Philip saith unto him, Lord, show us the Father, and it sufficeth us. Jesus saith unto him, Have I been so long time with you, and yet hast thou not known me, Philip? he that hath seen me hath seen the Father;

83. Jesus said: Images are visible to man but the light which is within them is hidden. The light of the father will be revealed, but he (his image) is hidden in the light.

84. Jesus said: When you see your reflection, you rejoice. Yet when you perceive your images which have come into being before you, which neither die nor can be seen, how much will you have to bear?

85. Jesus said: Adam came into existence from a great power and a great wealth, and yet he was not worthy of you. For if he had been worthy, he would not have tasted death.

86. Jesus said: The foxes have their dens and the birds have their nests, yet the Son of Man has no place to lay his head for rest.

Matthew 8:20 And Jesus said to him, Foxes have holes, and birds of the air have nests; but the Son of Man has nowhere to lay his head.

87. Jesus said: Wretched is the body which depends upon another body, and wretched is the soul which depends on these two (upon their being together).

88. Jesus said: The angels and the prophets will come to you, and what they will give you belongs to you. And you will give them what you have, and say among yourselves: When will they come to take (receive) what belongs to them?

89. Jesus said: Why do you wash the outside of your cup? Do you not understand (mind) that He who creates the inside is also He who creates the outside?

259

Luke 11:39-40 Then the Lord said to him, Now you Pharisees clean the outside of the cup and of the dish, but inside you are full of greed and wickedness. You fools! Did not the one who made the outside make the inside also?

90. Jesus said: Come unto me, for my yoke is comfortable (natural) and my lordship is gentle— and you will find rest for yourselves.

Matthew 11:28-30 Come to me, all you that are weary and are carrying heavy burdens, and I will give you rest. Take my yoke upon you, and learn from me; for I am gentle and humble in heart, and you will find rest for your souls. For my yoke is easy, and my burden is light.

Acts 15:5-17 But there rose up certain of the sect of the Pharisees which believed, saying, that it was needful to circumcise them, and to command them to keep the law of Moses. And the apostles and elders came together for to consider of this matter. And when there had been much disputing, Peter rose up, and said unto them, Men and brethren, ye know how that a good while ago God made choice among us, that the Gentiles by my mouth should hear the word of the gospel, and believe. And God, which knoweth the hearts, bare them witness, giving them the Holy Ghost, even as he did unto us. And put no difference between us and them, purifying their hearts by faith. Now therefore why tempt ye God, to put a yoke upon the neck of the disciples, which neither our fathers nor we were able to bear? But we believe that through the grace of the LORD Jesus Christ we shall be saved, even as they. Then all the multitude kept silence, and gave audience to Barnabas and Paul, declaring what miracles and wonders God had wrought among the Gentiles by them. And after they had held their peace, James answered, saying, Men and brethren, hearken unto me: Simeon hath declared how God at the first did visit the Gentiles, to take out of them a people for his name. And to this agree the words of the prophets; as it is written, After this I will return, and will build again the tabernacle of David, which is fallen down; and I will build again the ruins thereof, and I will set it up: That the residue of men might seek after the Lord, and all the Gentiles, upon whom my name is called, saith the Lord, who doeth all these things.

91. They said to him: Tell us who you are, so that we may believe in you. He said to them: You examine the face of the sky and of the earth, yet you do not recognize Him who is here with you, and you do not know how to seek in (to inquire of Him at) this moment (you do not know how to take advantage of this opportunity).

John 9:36 He answered, And who is he, sir? Tell me, so that I may believe in him.

Luke 12:54-56 He also said to the crowds, When you see a cloud rising in the west, you immediately say, It is going to rain; and so it happens. And when you see the south wind blowing, you say, There will be scorching heat; and it happens. You hypocrites! You know how to interpret the appearance of earth and sky, but why do you not know how to interpret the present time?

92. Jesus said: Seek and you will find. But in the past I did not answer the questions you asked. Now I wish to tell them to you, but you do not ask about (no longer seek) them.

Matthew 7:7 Ask, and it will be given you; search, and you will find; knock, and the door will be opened for you.

93. Jesus said: Do not give what is sacred to the dogs, lest they throw it on the dung heap. Do not cast the pearls to the swine, lest they cause it to become dung (mud).

Matthew 7:6 Do not give what is holy to dogs; and do not throw your pearls before swine, or they will trample them under foot and turn and maul you.

94. Jesus said: Whoever seeks will find. And whoever knocks, it will be opened to him.

Matthew 7:8 For everyone who asks receives, and everyone who searches finds, and for everyone who knocks, the door will be opened.

95. Jesus said: If you have money, do not lend at interest, but rather give it to those from whom you will not be repaid.

Luke 6:34-35 If you lend to those from whom you hope to receive, what credit is that to you? Even sinners lend to sinners, to receive as much again. But love your enemies, do good, and lend, expecting nothing in return. Your reward will be great, and you will be children of the Most High; for he is kind to the ungrateful and the wicked.

96. Jesus said: The Kingdom of the Father is like a woman who has taken a little yeast and hidden it in dough. She produced large loaves of it. Whoever has ears, let him hear!

Matthew 13:33 He told them another parable: The kingdom of heaven is like yeast that a woman took and mixed in with three measures of flour until all of it was leavened.

97. Jesus said: The Kingdom of the Father is like a woman who was carrying a jar full of grain. While she was walking on a road far from home, the handle of the jar broke and the grain poured out behind her onto the road. She did not know it. She had noticed no problem. When she arrived in her house, she set the jar down and found it empty.

98. Jesus said: The Kingdom of the Father is like someone who wished to slay a prominent person. While still in his own house he drew his sword and thrust it into the wall in order to test whether his hand would be strong enough. Then he slew the prominent person.

99. His Disciples said to him: Your brethren and your mother are standing outside. He said to them: Those here who do my Father's desires are my Brethren and my Mother. It is they who will enter the Kingdom of my Father.

Matthew 12:46-50 While he was still speaking to the crowds, his mother and his brothers were standing outside, wanting to speak to him. Someone told him, Look, your mother and your brothers are standing outside, wanting to speak to you. But to the one who had told him this, Jesus replied, Who is my mother, and who are my brothers? And pointing to his disciples, he said, Here are my mother and my brothers! For whoever does the will of my Father in heaven is my brother and sister and mother.

100. They showed Jesus a gold coin, and said to him: The agents of Caesar extort taxes from us. He said to them: Give the things of Caesar to Caesar, give the things of God to God, and give to me what is mine.

Mark 12:14-17 Is it lawful to pay taxes to the emperor, or not? Should we pay them, or should we not? But knowing their hypocrisy, he said to them, Why are you putting me to the test? Bring me a denarius and let me see it. And they brought one. Then he said to them, Whose head is this, and whose title? They answered, The emperor's. Jesus said to them, Give to the emperor the things that are the emperor's, and to God the things that are God's. And they were utterly amazed at him.

101. Jesus said: Whoever does not hate his father and his mother, as I do, will not be able to become my Disciple. And whoever does not love his father and his mother, as I do, will not be able to become my disciple. For my mother bore me, yet my true Mother gave me the life.

Matthew 10:37 Whoever loves father or mother more than me is not worthy of me; and whoever loves son or daughter more than me is not worthy of me.

102. Jesus said: Damn these Pharisees. They are like a dog sleeping in the feed trough of oxen. For neither does he eat, nor does he allow the oxen to eat.

Matthew 2:13 But woe unto you, scribes and Pharisees, hypocrites! because you shut the kingdom of heaven against men; for you neither enter yourselves, nor allow those who would enter to go in.

103. Jesus said: Blessed (happy) is the person who knows at what place of the house the bandits may break in, so that he can rise and collect his things and prepare himself before they enter.

Matthew 24:43 But understand this: if the owner of the house had known in what part of the night the thief was coming, he would have stayed awake and would not have let his house be broken into.

104. They said to him: Come, let us pray today and let us fast. Jesus said: What sin have I committed? How have I been overcome (undone)? When the Bridegroom comes forth from the bridal chamber, then let them fast and let them pray.

105. Jesus said: Whoever acknowledges (comes to know) father and mother, will be called the son of a whore.

106. Jesus said: When you make the two one, you will become Sons of Man (children of Adam), and when you say to the mountain: Move! It will move.

Mark 11:23 Truly I tell you, if you say to this mountain, Be taken up and thrown into the sea, and if you do not doubt in your heart, but believe that what you say will come to pass, it will be done for you.

107. Jesus said: The Kingdom is like a shepherd who has a hundred sheep. The largest one of them went astray. He left the ninety-nine and sought for the one until he found it. Having searched until he was weary, he said to that sheep: I desire you more than the ninety-nine.

Matthew 18:12-13 What do you think? If a shepherd has a hundred sheep, and one of them has gone astray, does he not leave the ninety-nine on the mountains and go in search of the one that went astray? And if he finds it, truly I tell you, he rejoices over it more than over the ninety-nine that never went astray.

108. Jesus said: Whoever drinks from my mouth will become like me. I will become him, and the secrets will be revealed to him.

109. Jesus said: The Kingdom is like a person who had a treasure hidden in his field and knew nothing of it. After he died, he bequeathed it to his son. The son accepted the field knowing nothing of the treasure. He sold it. Then the person who bought it came and plowed it. He found the treasure. He began to lend money at interest to whomever he wished.

Matthew 13:44 The kingdom of heaven is like treasure hidden in a field, which someone found and hid; then in his joy he goes and sells all that he has and buys that field.

110. Jesus said: Whoever has found the world (system) and becomes wealthy (enriched by it), let him renounce the world (system).

Mark 10:21-23 Then Jesus beholding him loved him, and said unto him, One thing thou lackest: go thy way, sell whatsoever thou hast, and give to the poor, and thou shalt have treasure in heaven: and come, take up the cross, and follow me. And he was sad at that saying, and went away grieved: for he had great possessions. And Jesus looked round about, and saith unto his disciples, How hardly shall they that have riches enter into the kingdom of God!

111. Jesus said: Heaven and earth will roll up (collapse and disappear) before you, but he who lives within the Living-One will neither see nor fear death. For, Jesus said: Whoever finds himself, of him the world is not worthy.

112. Jesus said: Damned is the flesh which depends upon the soul. Damned is the soul which depends upon the flesh.

113. His Disciples said to him: When will the Kingdom come? Jesus said: It will not come by expectation (because you watch or wait for it). They will not say: Look here! or: Look there! But the Kingdom of the Father is spread upon the earth, and people do not realize it.

Luke 17:20 And when he was demanded of by the Pharisees, when the kingdom of God should come, he answered them and said, The kingdom of God cometh not with observation: Neither shall they say, Lo-Here! Lo-There! For, behold, the kingdom of God is within you.

(Saying 114 was written later and was added to the original text.)

114. Simon Peter said to them: Send Mary away from us, for women are not worthy of this life. Jesus said: See, I will draw her into me so that I make her male, in order that she herself will become a living spirit like you males. For every female who becomes male will enter the Kingdom of the Heaven.

Joseph B. Lumpkin

Bibliography

The Scholars' Translation of the Gospel of Thomas
by Stephen Patterson and Marvin Meyer

The Complete Gospels: Annotated Scholars Version.*
Copyright 1992, 1994 by Polebridge Press

The Other Gospels: Non-Canonical Texts. Philadelphia:
Westminster, 1982.

The New Testament and Other Early Christian Writings: A
Reader. New York: Oxford University Press, 1998.

The Apocryphal New Testament. Oxford: Clarendon, 1993.

The Gospel of Thomas: The Hidden Sayings of Jesus. San
Fransisco: HarperCollins, 1992.

 Vol. 1 of New Testament Apocrypha. Westminster/John Knox,
1991.

Nag Hammadi Library In English. San Fransisco:
HarperCollins, 1988.

Nag Hammadi Codex II,2-7 Together With XIII,2*, BRIT. LIB.
OR. 4926(1), and P.OXY. 1, 654, 655. Vol. 1. New York: Brill,
1989.

The Greek Fragments.Nag Hammadi Codex II,2-7
Edited by Bentley Layton. Vol. 1. New York: Brill, 1989.
Critical Greek Text.

The Oxyrhynchus Logoi of Jesus and the Coptic Gospel According to Thomas. London: Geoffrey Chapman, 1971.

The Sayings of Jesus From Oxyrhynchus. Cambridge: Cambridge University Press, 1920.

New Sayings of Jesus. The Oxyrhynchus Papyri. London: Egypt Exploration Fund, 1904.

The Gospel of Philip : Jesus, Mary Magdalene, and the Gnosis of Sacred Union by Jean-Yves Leloup, Jacob Needleman, Inner Traditions (August 16, 2004)

The Gospel of Philip: Annotated & Explained by Andrew Philip Smith. Skylight Paths Publishing (August 30, 2005)

Lost Scriptures : Books That Did Not Make It Into The New Testament by Bart D. Ehrman. Oxford University Press, USA (October 2, 2003)

The Gnostic Gospels By Elaine Pagels. Vintage Books, January 1981

The Gnostic Gospels of Jesus. By Marvin Meyer. Harper San Francisco, 2005

Lost Christianities : The Battles for Scripture and the Faiths We Never Knew by Bart D. Ehrman. Oxford University Press, USA; New Ed edition (September 15, 2005)

The Gnostic Bible: Gnostic Texts of Mystical Wisdom from the Ancient and Medieval Worlds (Hardcover) by Willis Barnstone (Editor), Marvin Meyer (Editor). Shambhala; 1st edition (December 2, 2003)

The Gospel of Mary Magdalene by Jean-Yves Leloup, Jacob Needleman. Inner Traditions, March 30, 2002

The Gospel of Mary of Magdala: Jesus and the First Woman Apostle by Karen L. King. Polebridge Press November 2003

Various other sources.

ABOUT THE AUTHOR

Joseph Lumpkin has written for various newspapers and is the author of a number of books on the subjects of religion and philosophy including the best selling book, *The Lost Book Of Enoch: A Comprehensive Transliteration*, published by Fifth Estate Publishers.

Joseph holds his Doctorate in the field of Ministry. He lives near Birmingham, Alabama with his wife, Lynn, and his son, Breandan. He teaches, lectures, and writes as life allows.

Look for other fine books by Joseph Lumpkin.

The Lost Book Of Enoch: A Comprehensive Transliteration,
ISBN: 0974633666

The Gospel of Thomas: A Contemporary Translation
ISBN: 0976823349

Fallen Angels, The Watchers, and the Origins of Evil:
A Problem of Choice
ISBN: 1933580100

Dark Night of the Soul - A Journey to the Heart of God
ISBN: 0974633631

The Tao Te Ching: A Contemporary Translation
ISBN: 0976823314

Christian Counseling – Healing the Tribes of Man
ISBN: 1933589970

The Gnostic Gospels of Philip, Mary Magdalene, and Thomas:
Inside The Da Vinci Code and Holy Blood, Holy Grail
ISBN: 1933580135

The Book of Jubilees; The Little Genesis, The Apocalypse of Moses
ISBN: 1933580097

THE BOOK OF JASHER
The J. H. Parry Text in Modern English
ISBN: 1933580143

THE LOST BOOKS OF THE OLD TESTAMENT
ISBN: 1933580119

CPSIA information can be obtained
at www.ICGtesting.com
Printed in the USA
BVHW041537220921
617282BV00004B/229